A GUIDE TO

A VIEW FROM THE BRIDGE

SEAN SHEEHAN
WITH TONY BUZAN

Hodder & Stoughton

Cover photograph ©: The Ronald Grant Archive
Mind Maps: Ann Jones
Illustrations: Karen Donnelly

ISBN 0 340 75322 6

First published 1999
Impression number   10 9 8   7 6   5 4 3 2
Year   2002 2001 2000

Typeset by Transet Limited, Coventry, England.
Printed in Great Britain for Hodder & Stoughton Educational, a division of
Hodder Headline Plc, 338 Euston Road, London NW1 3BH by Cox and Wyman Ltd,
Reading, Berks.

CONTENTS

How to study   **v**

How to use this guide   **ix**

Key to icons   **xi**

Background   **1**

- The author   1
- Italian immigration   1
- How the play was written   2

The story of *A View from the Bridge*   **3**

Who's who?   **9**

- Eddie Carbone: Italian-American dock worker; married to Beatrice   9
- Catherine: 17 years old; brought up by Eddie and Beatrice   11
- Beatrice: Eddie's wife and Catherine's aunt   12
- Rodolpho: illegal Italian immigrant, younger brother to Marco   13
- Marco: Rodolpho's older brother, with wife and children in Italy   14
- Alfieri: lawyer in the Red Hook district where the dock workers live   14

Themes   18

- Justice and the law   18
- The parental role   19
- Marriage   20
- The American Dream   21
- Social codes   22

Commentary 26
- Act 1 27
- Act 2 49

Topics for discussion and brainstorming 71

How to get an 'A' in English Literature 74

The exam essay 75

Model answer and essay plan 76

Glossary of literary terms 80

Index 83

There are five important things you must know about your brain and memory to revolutionize
the way you study:

- ◆ how your memory
  ('recall') works *while* you are learning
- ◆ how your memory works *after* you have finished learning
- ◆ how to use Mind Maps – a special technique for helping you with all aspects of your studies
- ◆ how to increase your reading speed
- ◆ how to prepare for tests and exams.

Recall *during learning*
– THE NEED FOR BREAKS

When you are studying, your memory can concentrate, understand and remember well for between 20 and 45 minutes at a time. Then it needs a break. If you carry on for longer than this without a break your memory starts to break down. If you study for hours non-stop, you will remember only a small fraction of what you have been trying to learn, and you will have wasted hours of valuable time.

So, ideally, *study for less than an hour*, then take a five to ten minute break. During the break listen to music, go for a walk, do some exercise, or just daydream. (Daydreaming is a necessary brain-power booster – geniuses do it regularly.) During the break your brain will be sorting out what it has been learning, and you will go back to your books with the new information safely stored and organized in your memory banks. We recommend breaks at regular intervals as you work through the Literature Guides. Make sure you take them!

Recall after learning
– THE WAVES OF YOUR MEMORY

What do you think begins to happen to your
memory straight after you have finished learning something?
Does it immediately start forgetting? No! Your brain actually
increases its power and carries on remembering. For a short
time after your study session, your brain integrates the
information, making a more complete picture of everything it
has just learnt. Only then does the rapid decline in memory
begin, and as much as 80 per cent of what you have learnt can
be forgotten in a day.

However, if you catch the top of the wave of your memory,
and briefly review (look back over) what you have been
studying at the correct time, the memory is stamped in far more
strongly, and stays at the crest of the wave for a much longer
time. To maximize your brain's power to remember, take a few
minutes and use a Mind Map to review what you have learnt
at the end of a day. Then review it at the end of a week, again
at the end of a month, and finally a week before your test or
exam. That way you'll ride your memory
wave all the way there – and beyond!

The Mind Map ®
– A PICTURE OF THE WAY YOU THINK

Do you like taking notes? More importantly, do you like having to
go back over and learn them before tests or exams? Most
students I know certainly do not! And how do you take your
notes? Most people take notes on lined paper, using blue or
black ink. The result, visually, is boring! And what does *your*
brain do when it is bored? It turns off, tunes out, and goes to
sleep! Add a dash of colour, rhythm, imagination, and the whole
note-taking process becomes much more fun, uses more of your
brain's abilities, and improves your recall and understanding.

A Mind Map mirrors the way your brain works. It can be used
for note-taking from books or in class, for reviewing what you
have just studied, and for essay planning for coursework and
in tests or exams. It uses all your memory's natural techniques
to build up your rapidly growing 'memory muscle'.

You will find Mind Maps throughout this book. Study them, add some colour, personalize them, and then have a go at drawing your own – you'll remember them far better! Stick them in your files and on your walls for a quick-and-easy review of the topic.

HOW TO DRAW A MIND MAP

1 Start in the middle of the page. This gives your brain the maximum room for its thoughts.
2 Always start by drawing a small picture or symbol. Why? Because a picture is worth a thousand words to your brain. And try to use at least three colours, as colour helps your memory even more.
3 Let your thoughts flow, and write or draw your ideas on coloured branching lines connected to your central image. These key symbols and words are the headings for your topic. Start like the Mind Map on page 9.
4 Then add facts and ideas by drawing more, smaller, branches on to the appropriate main branches, just like a tree.
5 Always print your word clearly on its line. Use only one word per line.
6 To link ideas and thoughts on different branches, use arrows, colours, underlining, and boxes (see page 17).

HOW TO READ A MIND MAP

1 Begin in the centre, the focus of your topic.
2 The words/images attached to the centre are like chapter headings; read them next.
3 Always read out from the centre, in every direction (even on the left-hand side, where you will have to read from right to left, instead of the usual left to right).

USING MIND MAPS

Mind Maps are a versatile tool – use them for taking notes in class or from books, for solving problems, for brainstorming with friends, and for reviewing and working for tests or exams – their uses are endless! You will find them invaluable for planning essays for coursework and exams. Number your main branches in the order in which you want to use them and off you go – the main headings for your essay are done and all your ideas are logically organized!

Super speed reading

It seems incredible, but it's been proved – the faster you read, the more you understand and remember! So here are some tips to help you to practise reading faster – you'll cover the ground more quickly, remember more, and have more time left for both work and play.

◆ First read the whole text (whether it's a lengthy book or an exam or test paper) very quickly, to give your brain an overall idea of what's ahead and get it working. (It's like sending out a scout to look at the territory you have to cover – it's much easier when you know what to expect!) Then read the text again for more detailed information.

◆ Have the text a reasonable distance away from your eyes. In this way your eye/brain system will be able to see more at a glance, and will naturally begin to read faster.

◆ Take in groups of words at a time. Rather than reading 'slowly and carefully' read faster, more enthusiastically.

◆ Take in phrases rather than single words while you read.

◆ Use a guide. Your eyes are designed to follow movement, so a thin pencil underneath the lines you are reading, moved smoothly along, will 'pull' your eyes to faster speeds.

Preparing for tests and exams

◆ Review your work systematically. Cram at the start of your course, not the end, and avoid 'exam panic'!

◆ Use Mind Maps throughout your course, and build a Master Mind Map for each subject – a giant Mind Map that summarises everything you know about the subject.

◆ Use memory techniques such as mnemonics (verses or systems for remembering things like dates and events).

◆ Get together with one or two friends to study, compare Mind Maps, and discuss topics.

AND FINALLY...

Have *fun* while you learn – it has been shown that students who make their studies enjoyable understand and remember everything better and get the highest grades. I wish you and your brain every success! (Tony Buzan)

This guide assumes that you have already read *A View from the Bridge*, although you could read 'Background' and 'The story of *A View from the Bridge*' before that. It is best to use the guide alongside the play. You could read the 'Who's Who?' and 'Themes' sections without referring to the play, but you will get more out of these sections if you do refer to it to check the points made in these sections, and especially when thinking about the questions designed to test your recall and help you to think about the play.

THE DIFFERENT SECTIONS

The 'Commentary' section can be used in a number of ways. One way is to read a section in the play, and then read the Commentary for that scene. Keep on until you come to a test section, test yourself – then have a break! Alternatively, read the Commentary for a scene, then read that scene in the play, then go back to the Commentary. Find out what works best for you.

'Topics for discussion and brainstorming' gives topics that could well feature in exams or provide the basis for coursework. It would be particularly useful for you to discuss them with friends, or brainstorm them using Mind Map techniques (see p. vi).

'How to get an "A" in English Literature' gives valuable advice on what to look for in a text, and what skills you need to develop in order to achieve your personal best.

'The exam essay' is a useful 'night before' reminder of how to tackle exam questions, and 'Model answer' gives an example of an A-grade essay and the Mind Map and plan used to write it.

THE QUESTIONS

Whenever you come across a question in the guide with a star ❂ in front of it, think about it for a moment. You could even jot down a few words in rough to focus your mind. There is not usually a 'right' answer to these questions: it is important for you to develop your own opinions if you want to get an 'A' in your exam. The 'Test yourself' sections are designed to take you about 10–20 minutes each – which will be time well spent. Take a short break after each one.

PAGE NUMBERS

Page references are to the Penguin edition. If you have another edition, the page numbers may be slightly different.

KEY TO ICONS

*T*hemes

A **theme** is an idea explored by an author. Whenever a theme is dealt with in the guide, the appropriate icon is used. This means you can find where a theme is just by flicking through the book. Go on – try it now!

- Justice and the law

- The parental role

- Marriage

- The American Dream

- Social codes

 STYLE AND LANGUAGE

This heading and icon are used in the 'Commentary' wherever there is a special section on the author's choice of words and **imagery**.

The author

Two generations before he was born in 1915 Arthur Miller's family had emigrated from Poland to America. Miller was born in New York and after the fortunes of his family suffered during the years of economic depression they moved to the working-class district of Brooklyn. As a teenager Miller worked to save money so that he could afford to attend university and although he first studied economics and history he later changed to English. After graduating from university he worked as a journalist and began writing plays but he also worked in the Brooklyn shipyards for two years and met many Italian workers and their families. It was this experience that gave him the idea of writing *A View from the Bridge* and the original story upon which he based his play was first told to Arthur Miller by a longshoreman.

Italian immigration

Miller learnt a lot about the struggles of Italian immigrants when he worked in the shipyards. He learnt of the terrible poverty that drove them to leave their own country and how they were often forced to leave their families behind in Italy. Sicily, where many of the poorer immigrants came from, was one of the most desperately deprived areas in the whole of Europe and Miller later travelled there to see the place for himself. He also learnt of the struggles that faced them when they arrived in New York. They had to adapt to a new culture and because they were poor and powerless they were open to exploitation, especially when it came to finding work. They had to wait at the docks hoping to find employment and they had very few rights, especially if they were illegal immigrants. Miller, learning from their experiences, came to understand how important the Italian community was to the men and women who struggled to find a new life in America. It was only in their own communities where they lived with fellow Italians that they gained the self-respect that was so vital in helping them to endure the injustice and humiliation of being exploited and poorly paid. Miller himself became a socialist and his most famous play, *The Crucible*, was a reaction to the hysteria and fear that was whipped up by politicians against people with left-wing sympathies.

How the play was written

A View from the Bridge was first written as a one-act play in verse and produced in 1955 in New York. It was not a great success and Miller dropped the verse-form and made other changes before the play appeared on the stage in London as a two-act play in 1956. Miller has spoken about what attracted him to the story and why he decided to make a play out of it. He was interested in the tale of someone who can be driven to make 'a sacrifice of himself for his conception, however misguided, of right, dignity and justice'. Around this time Miller divorced his first wife and married the actress Marilyn Monroe but this relationship also ended in divorce in 1961.

THE STORY OF *A VIEW FROM THE BRIDGE*

Act 1

Alfieri, a lawyer sympathetic to the Italian immigrant families struggling to survive, introduces the audience to the Red Hook area of Brooklyn, a **close-knit** Italian-American community in New York. **Eddie Carbone** lives in Red Hook with his wife, **Beatrice**, and her niece **Catherine**. Eddie, who is **possessive** about Catherine, is concerned that she is about to leave school and start work. News comes that two cousins of Beatrice, **illegal immigrants**, have just arrived on a ship. Eddie reminds them of Vinny Bolzano, a man punished by his own family for informing the Immigration Bureau of illegal Italian immigrants. A strict **code of society** operates in this close-knit community, a code that is not always in harmony with the actual law.

The cousins, **Marco** and his younger brother **Rodolpho**, are welcomed and they talk of their hopes for the future and their understanding of the **American Dream**. Eddie, however, quickly takes a dislike to Rodolpho. He notices the growing **attraction** between him and Catherine and becomes **jealous**. He tells Catherine that Rodolpho is using her to gain an American passport but she does not believe him. Beatrice, concerned at her husband's growing possessiveness, advises her niece to act more independently.

Eddie visits Alfieri only to be told that Rodolpho has broken no law other than his act of illegally entering the country. At home, the growing **intimacy** between **Catherine** and **Rodolpho** causes Eddie to make his displeasure felt. Catherine, however, asserts her independence by dancing with Rodolpho in the room of their apartment. Eddie, with the excuse of teaching Rodolpho how to box, hits him fairly hard. Marco then challenges Eddie to a chair-lifting contest and beats him easily. Act 1 ends with Marco holding a chair above Eddie's head and looking directly into his face; a clear warning to Eddie not to bully his brother.

Act 2

Eddie returns home drunk to find Rodolpho with Catherine in the bedroom. He orders Rodolpho out of his home but when Catherine threatens to leave with him Eddie grabs hold of her and **kisses** her. He provokes Rodolpho into trying to attack him and then kisses him as well.

A few days later Eddie visits Alfieri who tries to get him to see sense and accept that Catherine must make her own decisions. He knows that Eddie could inform the immigration authorities and warns him that this would lose him friends and the respect of the community. Eddie does not listen and **informs** on his wife's cousins.

Marco and Rodolpho are arrested and, although Eddie denies the fact, Beatrice and Catherine and Marco all realize who is responsible. Marco **accuses** him in front of neighbours so that everyone knows that Eddie has broken the code of their society. Marco accuses Eddie of effectively killing his children because he can no longer send money home to Italy. His children will go without food and Eddie is seen to be responsible. There is a need for **justice** but the law cannot do anything; quite the opposite, in fact, because the law would approve of Eddie reporting a breach of the immigration laws.

Marco is allowed out of prison on **bail** after he reluctantly promises Alfieri not to attack Eddie. Rodolpho and Catherine will marry as planned and this will allow Marco's younger brother to stay in America. Marco himself knows he will be sent back.

On the day of the wedding Beatrice is told by her husband not to come home if she insists on attending the wedding. Rodolpho arrives with the warning that Marco is on his way and apologizes to Eddie in the hope that he will leave before his brother arrives.

Eddie refuses to leave. He **accuses Marco** of lying and in the **fight** that follows Eddie is **killed** by the knife that he draws on Marco. Alfieri draws the play to an end and mourns the death of a man who, however wrongly, 'allowed himself to be wholly known'.

HOW WELL HAVE YOU REMEMBERED THE PLOT?

Try to fill in the words missing from this summary without looking at the original. Feel free to use your own words if they have the same meaning.

Act 1

_____, a lawyer sympathetic to the Italian immigrant families struggling to survive, introduces the audience to the Red Hook area of Brooklyn, a _____ Italian-American community in New York. _____ _____ lives in Red Hook with his wife, _____, and her niece _____. Eddie, who is _____ about Catherine, is concerned that she is about to leave school and start work. News comes that two cousins of Beatrice, _____ _____, have just arrived on a ship. Eddie reminds them of Vinny Bolzano, a man punished by his own family for informing the Immigration Bureau of illegal Italian immigrants. A strict _____ _____ _____ operates in this close-knit community, a code that is not always in harmony with the actual law.

The cousins, _____ and his younger brother _____, are welcomed and they talk of their hopes for the future and their understanding of the _____ _____. Eddie, however, quickly takes a dislike to Rodolpho. He notices the growing _____ between him and Catherine and becomes _____. He tells Catherine that Rodolpho is only using her to gain an American passport but she does not believe him. Beatrice, concerned at her husband's growing possessiveness, advises her niece to act more independently.

Eddie visits Alfieri only to be told that Rodolpho has broken no law other than his act of illegally entering the country. At home, the growing _____ between _____ and _____ causes Eddie to make his displeasure felt. Catherine, however, asserts her independence by dancing with Rodolpho in the room of their apartment. Eddie, with the excuse of teaching Rodolpho how to box, hits him fairly hard. Marco then challenges Eddie to a chair-lifting contest and beats him easily. Act 1 ends with Marco holding a chair above Eddie's head and looking directly into his face; a clear warning to Eddie not to bully his brother.

5

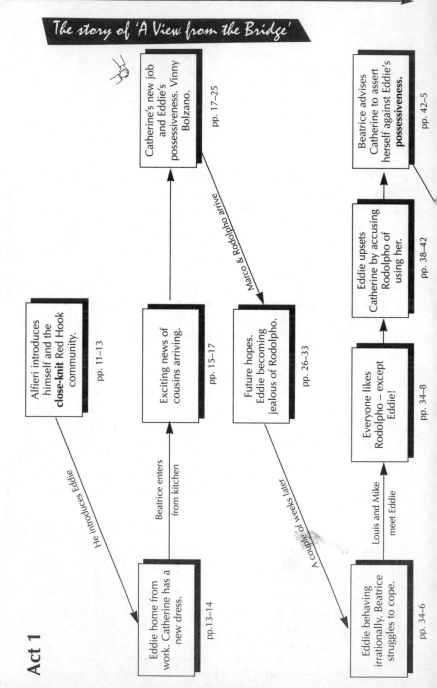

The story of 'A View from the Bridge'

Act 1

Alfieri introduces himself and the **close-knit** Red Hook community.

pp. 11–13

He introduces Eddie

Eddie home from work. Catherine has a new dress.

pp.13–14

Beatrice enters from kitchen

Exciting news of cousins arriving.

pp. 15–17

Catherine's new job and Eddie's possessiveness. Vinny Bolzano.

pp. 17–25

Marco & Rodolpho arrive

Future hopes. Eddie becoming jealous of Rodolpho.

pp. 26–33

A couple of weeks later

Eddie behaving irrationally. Beatrice struggles to cope.

pp. 34–6

Louis and Mike meet Eddie

Everyone likes Rodolpho – except Eddie!

pp. 34–8

Eddie upsets Catherine by accusing Rodolpho of using her.

pp. 38–42

Beatrice advises Catherine to assert herself against Eddie's **possessiveness.**

pp. 42–5

6

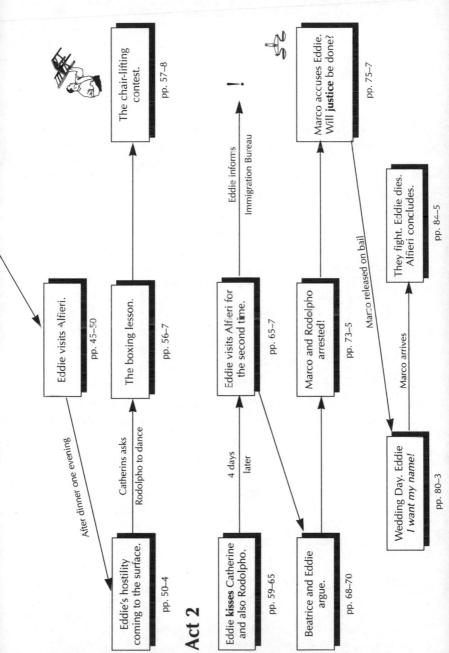

Eddie visits Alfieri.
pp. 45–50

The chair-lifting contest.
pp. 57–8

The boxing lesson.
pp. 56–7

Catherine asks Rodolpho to dance

After dinner one evening

Eddie's hostility coming to the surface.
pp. 50–4

Act 2

Eddie **kisses** Catherine and also Rodolpho.
pp. 59–65

4 days later

Eddie visits Alfieri for the second time.
pp. 65–7

Eddie informs Immigration Bureau

Marco and Rodolpho arrested!
pp. 73–5

Beatrice and Eddie argue.
pp. 68–70

Marco accuses Eddie. Will **justice** be done?
pp. 75–7

Marco released on bail

Wedding Day. Eddie. *I want my name!*
pp. 80–3

Marco arrives

They fight. Eddie dies. Alfieri concludes.
pp. 84–5

7

Act 2

Eddie returns home drunk to find Rodolpho with Catherine in the bedroom. He orders Rodolpho out of his home but when Catherine threatens to leave with him Eddie grabs hold of her and _____ her. He provokes Rodolpho into trying to attack him and then kisses him as well.

A few days later Eddie visits Alfieri who tries to get him to see sense and accept that Catherine must make her own decisions. He knows that Eddie could inform the immigration authorities and warns him that this would lose him friends and the respect of the community. Eddie does not listen and _____ on his wife's cousins.

Marco and Rodolpho are arrested and, although Eddie denies the fact, Beatrice and Catherine and Marco all realize who is responsible. Marco _____ him in front of neighbours so that everyone knows that Eddie has broken the code of their society. Marco accuses Eddie of effectively killing his children because he can no longer send money home to Italy. His children will go without food and Eddie is seen to be responsible. There is a need for _____ but the law cannot do anything; quite the opposite, in fact, because the law would approve of Eddie reporting a breach of the immigration laws.

_____ is allowed out of prison on _____ after he reluctantly promises Alfieri not to attack Eddie. Rodolpho and Catherine will marry as planned and this will allow Marco's younger brother to stay in America. Marco himself knows he will be sent back.

On the day of the wedding Beatrice is told by her husband not to come home if she insists on attending the wedding. Rodolpho arrives with the warning that Marco is on his way and apologizes to Eddie in the hope that he will leave before his brother arrives.

Eddie refuses to leave. He _____ _____ of lying and in the _____ that follows Eddie is _____ by the knife that he draws on Marco. Alfieri draws the play to an end and mourns the death of a man who, however wrongly, 'allowed himself to be wholly known'.

The Mini Mind Map above summarizes the main characters in *A View from the Bridge*. When you have read this section, look at the full Mind Map on p. 17, then make a copy of the Mini Mind Map and try to add to it from memory.

Eddie

Eddie is the central character in the play. In different ways he relates to everyone else in the story and it is his behaviour that drives forward the action of the drama.

He is a very forceful person who sees himself in the traditional role of the male breadwinner, the head of the household, and he is used to getting his own way. His possessiveness towards his niece Catherine is seen when he lectures her about wearing a short skirt and *walkin' wavvy*. When he is told about her offer of a job his first reaction is negative and only reluctantly is he persuaded to accept the situation. He wants things to remain the same and finds it difficult to accept change. The darker aspect of his possessiveness comes to the surface when Rodolpho and Catherine fall in love. He convinces himself that Rodolpho is as an effeminate homosexual who is exploiting Catherine in order to legalize his presence in America but the suspicion that this is all an excuse to disguise his jealousy grows stronger as events unfold.

Eddie becomes increasingly irrational at the thought of losing Catherine. The scene where he kisses Catherine and Rodolpho brings out the confused state of his sexual feelings. By kissing Rodolpho he is deliberately insulting him and accusing him of homosexuality but Eddie is also driven by sexual feelings of his own and by kissing Catherine he betrays how he feels about her, although he will not admit this to himself. He drives himself into a state of despair and finally informs on his wife's cousins to the immigration authorities. ✪ Do you think Eddie realizes that he has behaved like Vinny Bolzano?

His forceful and demanding personality is also apparent in his relationship with his wife. He expects her to always agree with him, and he becomes increasingly angry when she fails to share his opinion of Rodolpho.

There is a warmer side to Eddie and we catch glimpses of this in the course of the play. He is a man who has worked hard for his wife and niece, and he has a strong sense of community. He welcomes his wife's cousins into his home and when he is explaining why he is happy to help them he speaks of it as being honourable behaviour (p. 17). He is very aware of his society's code of behaviour. Unfortunately, the powerful passion that drives him into a state of irrational jealousy finally destroys him. In his society, his act of betrayal is seen as a crime and his showdown with Marco is a desperate attempt to regain his sense of honour and the respect of his community. When he faces Marco at the end of the play he has blocked out the fact that he made the fateful telephone call and never admits that he wants Catherine to himself.

What finally matters most to Eddie is his loss of face, his loss of self, when he is judged and condemned by the code of the society in which he has found an identity. He was someone once; he had family and friends, but he ends up facing a future as a *nobody*. He cries out *'I want my name'*, and although he has not admitted the truth to himself there is something noble about the way Eddie faces death in a desperate attempt to put back the clock. He never wanted things to change and he dies trying to become the Eddie Carbone, the streetwise Italian-American longshoreman, of the past: *'Yeah, Marco! Eddie Carbone. Eddie Carbone. Eddie Carbone.'* ✪ How do you feel towards Eddie at the end of the play? Can you sympathize with him?

Catherine

Catherine has grown up in a loving and warm relationship with her aunt and uncle. This is apparent in the first scene before the arrival of the immigrants where her innocence and trust are demonstrated. The arrival of Rodolpho changes everything because her growing love for him brings out a passionate jealousy in her uncle that her limited experience prevents her from understanding. In the course of the play she learns a great deal and grows up in the process. ✪ Can you remember how you first felt about Catherine in the opening scenes of the play?

After a talk with her aunt Catherine has some awareness of the need to distance herself from Eddie. She tells Rodolpho how unhappy she is to see Eddie becoming unlikeable because she has such heart-warming memories of their past happiness. She explains this to Rodolpho: *'You think it's so easy to turn around and say to a man he's nothin' to you no more?'* This shows the warm and compassionate side of her nature.

Catherine is shocked in the scene where Eddie kisses her and then Rodolpho, and it changes her attitude towards her uncle. She is very much in love with Rodolpho and learns to trust him instead of Eddie. She allows herself to be persuaded by Beatrice into inviting Eddie to her marriage but his act of betrayal destroys the remaining bond between them. When she calls him a *rat* who *bites people when they sleep* she is no longer the trusting niece who loved him like a father. By the end of the play she has grown up in a very short time and become more independent and self-aware. Her final words to Eddie are ones of regret: *'Eddie, I never meant to do anything bad to you.'*

Of all the characters in the play Catherine is the one who changes most as a result of what happens. Her accelerated progress into adult life brings the prospect of a loving future life with Rodolpho but her happy years of childhood are abruptly brought to a violent and unhappy end. ✪ In what way do you think Catherine might be thought to bear some of the responsibility for what has happened to Eddie? Or do you think her early innocence makes it unfair to suggest she should bear some of the responsibility?

Beatrice

Beatrice is a loving wife to Eddie and a caring aunt to Catherine. The early scene around the dinner table with her husband and niece brings out her good sense and her consideration for others. When Catherine wants to tell Eddie about her new job, Beatrice senses that he might not approve and says, '*Let him eat first, then we'll tell him.*' She handles her husband's objections with diplomacy and, while she never becomes angry, she is capable of being direct and honest: '*...you gonna keep her in the house all her life?*'

Beatrice is worried by the way Rodolpho's arrival affects her husband and she talks to Catherine and advises her to distance herself from Eddie. She senses that her husband's feelings for Catherine are more than those of a protective father-figure. She also tries to advise Eddie about respecting their niece's independence. Beatrice also gently confronts her husband with the fact that they no longer make love. This shows us how she sensibly attempts to deal with difficulties. ✪ Do you think it is fair to say that Beatrice is partly to blame for the unhappy state of their married life?

As her husband's behaviour becomes increasingly irrational, Beatrice finds it more difficult to reason with him. '*What do you want from me? They've moved out, what do you want now?*', she asks after moving her cousins out of their apartment. She is terribly shocked by the realization that Eddie has informed on them. Beatrice, however, is very loyal to her husband and when he forces her to choose between staying with him or going to the wedding she has no difficulty about deciding to remain with him.

Beatrice confronts Eddie with the truth about his feelings for Catherine when she is desperate to prevent them fighting: '*The truth is not as bad as blood, Eddie! I'm tellin' you the truth – tell her good-bye for ever!*' ✪ Do you think this is something Beatrice should have said a lot earlier to Eddie?

A reconciliation of sorts occurs at the end of the play when Eddie dies in the arms of his wife. Beatrice is the last thought on his mind, a reminder that for many years their relationship was a strong and loving one.

Rodolpho

Rodolpho has accompanied his older brother, Marco, to America. His youthful personality and cheerful ways endear him to everyone he meets, except Eddie of course. Catherine and Beatrice warm to him immediately and there is no suggestion that Eddie is right when he accuses him of using Catherine to obtain American citizenship. A conversation between Louis and Mike, two longshoremen who work with him, testifies to his winning manner: '*You take one look at him – everybody's happy.*' This tells us that Rodolpho is genuinely liked by other people and helps convince the audience that there is no truth to Eddie's wild speculations about his sexuality.

Rodolpho can cook, and sing, and make clothes and there is reason to believe him when he tells Catherine: '*If I were not afraid to be arrested I would start to be something wonderful here!*' These words are from the scene that open Act 2, an important scene for understanding that there is far more to Rodolpho than just good looks and a sense of humour. He convinces Catherine, and the audience, that he really loves her, and his own strong sense of dignity comes across. Rodolpho is intelligent and this is shown by his ability not to be taken in by the American Dream: '*You think we have no tall buildings in Italy?.... Only work we don't have. I want to be an American so I can work...*'

Rodolpho's sensitivity and good nature is also revealed towards the end of the play when he returns to warn Eddie that Marco is on his way. Despite what Eddie has done to him and his brother, he is anxious to avoid bloodshed and his apology to Eddie is heartfelt and balanced.

When Rodolpho first appears with his older brother it is possible to see him as immature and a little silly. By the end of the play he has shown himself to be mature and responsible. Like Catherine, perhaps, he has been forced to grow up quickly but there is every reason to think that he will be a sensible and considerate adult. ❂ Do you agree with this or do you think he has swept Catherine off her feet and that later their relationship may not prove to be so strong?

Marco

For most of the play, Marco is focused on the task of providing for his wife and family back in Italy. He is a serious man who has come to America for the sole purpose of trying to earn money for his family. He is aware of the kindness shown by Beatrice and Eddie in accommodating him and his brother and is very grateful for their help. The chair-lifting competition that brings Act 1 to an end shows that he has a protective attitude towards his younger brother and that he will not allow him to be bullied by anyone.

Marco has a strong awareness of his society's code of behaviour and this is something he shares with Eddie. When he realizes that Eddie has betrayed them to the immigration authorities he is in no doubt that this is something that cannot go unpunished. When Alfieri is trying to persuade him to promise not to go after Eddie he at first refuses because *such a promise is dishonourable*. When the lawyer explains that Eddie cannot be punished by the law for what he has done, Marco replies 'All the law is not in a book.' Marco believes in a concept of justice that can override whatever the law might say. When Eddie is seen to have behaved unjustly, Marco comes after him like an avenging angel. ✪ Is it obvious that Marco came after Eddie with the intention of killing him? Or does Miller leave this open for the audience to decide?

Marco pursues Eddie because he sees this as his duty, the only honourable way for a man to behave in the circumstances. When, in the opening speech of the play, Alfieri spoke of how Italian-Americans can now *settle for half* he did not have people like Marco in mind. Marco comes from an older society where scores are settled using violence. ✪ How do you feel about Marco at the end of the play? Did he have a choice over how to react to Eddie's betrayal?

Alfieri

Alfieri is different from the other characters in the play because his role includes that of a commentator who views the whole drama and speaks directly to the audience.

Alfieri is also a character in the play because Eddie comes to him for advice and he is also involved in getting Marco out of prison on bail. As a character involved in the action of the play, he is a lawyer who understands the plight of Italian-Americans and illegal Italian immigrants. He tells Eddie, and later Marco, what the law can and cannot do but he is also sympathetic and tries to offer sensible advice. As a lawyer, he represents the law but he knows that the law cannot always match people's sense of justice. ❂ Can you think of a modern example where you feel the law does not match the needs of justice?

Alfieri's most important role is as a commentator who views the human drama unfolding while relating it to broader ideas. It is Alfieri who stands on the bridge between the two types of justice and observes the drama; it is he who offers a 'view from the bridge', which is also, more literally the Brooklyn Bridge. In his opening speech he talks of the conflict between the claims of the law and an older, more traditional, sense of right and wrong. It is Alfieri who draws our attention to this important **theme**.

It is Alfieri who makes the story of Eddie Carbone into something more than just the tale of an older man who destroys himself because of a passionate attachment to his young niece. He relates the story to a broader sense of history and to a sense of how a society can have its own code of behaviour which can prove stronger than the law itself. Alfieri lets us see how Eddie and Marco are almost conditioned by their society into thinking the way they do and this helps us to understand the tragedy that enfolds them. Alfieri creates a sense of inevitability which suggests the individual characters are caught up with forces, social and emotional ones, that they cannot control.

In ancient Greek **tragedy**, the **chorus** is a group of figures who comment on and express feelings about what is happening. They usually speak about the drama in a style different from that of the characters involved in the action. Alfieri has this choral dimension to his role. As a commentator, he speaks differently from the other characters and his role is to remind the audience of the broader significance of what is happening.

Know yourself

You deserve a break after reading through the 'Who's who?' section but let's finish with *your* thoughts and not just those of the author of this guide.

?   The characters in the play show different levels of self-awareness and while some of them come to a deeper understanding about themselves, others are more or less the same at the end as they were in the beginning. Think about this for yourself and place marks on the lines below to indicate the level of self-awareness at the start and end of the play.

START	SELF-AWARENESS	END

LOW ———————————— HIGH| Eddie |LOW ———————————— HIGH

LOW ———————————— HIGH| Catherine |LOW ———————————— HIGH

LOW ———————————— HIGH| Beatrice |LOW ———————————— HIGH

LOW ———————————— HIGH| Rodolpho |LOW ———————————— HIGH

LOW ———————————— HIGH| Marco |LOW ———————————— HIGH

LOW ———————————— HIGH| Alfieri |LOW ———————————— HIGH

?   Think about the following statements and mark each one **T**rue or **F**alse.

There is nothing about Eddie to admire.

Rodolpho and Catherine are more honest with each other than Eddie and Beatrice.

Alfieri is the only character who can stand back and have 'a view from the bridge'.

Rodolpho and Marco share the same values and are the same kind of people.

Now you have earned a break. Enjoy!

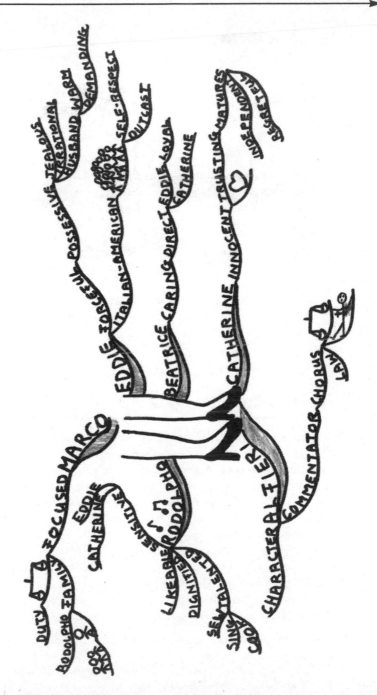

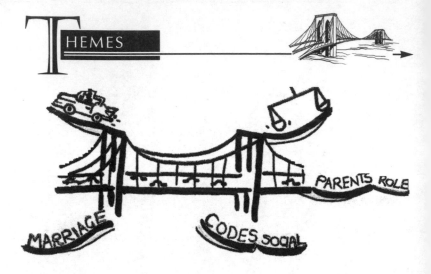

THEMES

A **theme** is an idea which runs through a work and which is
explored and developed along the way. The Mini Mind Map
above shows the main themes of *A View from the Bridge*. Test
yourself by copying the Mini Mind Map, and then try adding to
it before comparing your results with the version on p. 25.

Justice and the law

The theme of justice and the law, exploring how they can
come into conflict with one another, is introduced at the
beginning of the play. Alfieri contrasts the past with the present
to bring out different equations between justice and the law.
On one side we have a play set in modern New York, where
there are laws and policemen. On the other side we have an
Italian-American community which shares an older tradition,
one that insists on justice, as seen by the community, being
carried out whether the law allows it or not. This tradition is
traced back to ancient Sicily and Alfieri also sees it at work in
the gun battles that broke out on the streets of New York,
involving figures like Al Capone.

Alfieri speaks of his present generation as a society *quite
civilized, quite American* and this is because *we settle for half.*
By accepting a set of laws, he sees society as having agreed to

play by the rules even when the rules are seen as unfair. He points out to Eddie that Rodolpho is not breaking any law and therefore he has to accept this. Eddie has so convinced himself that Rodolpho is unfairly using Catherine that he sees this as unjust. He is annoyed that the law cannot do anything about it.

Alfieri also advises Marco about what the law can and cannot do. Eddie has not broken any law by phoning the immigration authorities, quite the opposite in fact. Marco cannot accept this, it breaks an older unwritten law, and he is driven to carry out justice as he sees fit. This way of viewing justice lies behind the story of Vinny Bolzano, someone punished by his community for committing what is seen as a social crime.

The tragedy of Eddie and Marco is that they cannot escape this tradition. By the end of the play Eddie is convinced he has been unfairly treated and he demands justice. Marco is also demanding justice. They cannot compromise. At the end, even though there is something he admires about Eddie, he sees that *it is better to settle for half, it must be!*

The parental role

Eddie is not Catherine's father but he fulfils the parental role in her life and it is a vital aspect of their relationship. *A View from the Bridge* explores the parental role and examines the way in which it can blur the boundary between protectiveness and possessiveness. This theme can be traced in three stages: at the beginning of the play, in the scenes following Rodolpho's arrival, and after Eddie's telephone call to the immigration authorities.

Eddie and Catherine are first seen in a friendly and warm relationship and the audience senses that this has been built up over the years since Catherine was a little girl. Eddie reminds her that he has a duty to protect her. *'I'm responsible for you,'* he tells her, but his disapproval of her new job confirms the possessive nature of his attachment to his niece. Catherine is on the threshold of her adult life and instead of being supportive Eddie is uncomfortable with the situation. He wants to maintain the role of being a father figure to a little girl who adores and trusts him.

The developing love between Catherine and Rodolpho makes Eddie increasingly irrational as he tries to convince others that Rodolpho is not to be trusted. By allowing his own emotional and sexual feelings to influence his behaviour Eddie exceeds the responsibilities of the parental role.

Beatrice realizes that her husband has become too emotionally involved in the role of caring for her niece. She speaks to Catherine who herself gradually becomes aware of the need to pull herself away from her uncle. This becomes an emotional tug of war which fractures their family life and finally leads to tragedy.

When Eddie informs the immigration authorities he betrays not only Rodolpho but his own responsibility as a father figure to accept the independence of someone who is growing into adulthood. Eddie betrays the trust that had built up between them and the result is a terrible bitterness.

She turns on him, calls him a rat and dismisses him with contempt: '*In the garbage he belongs!*' In a desperate attempt to save him, Beatrice confronts him with the truth that he has always denied: '*You want somethin' else, Eddie, and you can never have her!*'

Marriage

The audience gets a glimpse of the warm relationship that once existed between Beatrice and her husband when Eddie says it is an honour to help her cousins. Tears comes to her eyes as she turns proudly to Catherine and says '*You see what he is?…You're an angel!*' For most of the play, however, the audience views a marriage under increasing stress.

The pressure comes from Eddie's irrational attitude towards Rodolpho and Beatrice's gradual realization that her husband cannot let Catherine go. Beatrice finds this difficult to cope with and makes clear to her husband how stressed she is by what is happening: '*You going to leave her alone? Or you gonna drive me crazy?*' Eddie walks out of the apartment after this and Beatrice then tries to deal with it by advising Catherine to assert her independence from Eddie.

Beatrice continues to hope that she can save their marriage. When Eddie begins the boxing lesson Beatrice convinces herself that it is just harmless fun. By the end of the 'lesson' she has to push Eddie into his armchair when she realizes he wanted to hurt Rodolpho. Later she moves her cousins into a separate flat in the hope that this will help matters.

Beatrice is deeply disturbed by her husband's act of betrayal and can hardly believe what he has done. She remains loyal, however, when Eddie makes her choose between staying with him or leaving to attend the wedding. Eddie expects a wife to be obedient but Beatrice does not stay with him out of some simple notion of wifely duty.

When Catherine turns on Eddie and calls him a rat, Beatrice tries to defend her husband: '*Whatever happened we all done it.*' She sees herself as being partly responsible, perhaps because she feels that she allowed her husband and niece to become too close. ✪ How much of the blame do you feel she deserves.

As Eddie prepares to meet Marco the audience is moved by Beatrice's desperate attempt to protect her husband: '*Listen to me, I love you, I'm talkin' to you.*' Eddie does not listen. In the end, his need to try to regain some respect from his society proves too strong. Only at the end, when he lays dying, does Eddie allow his thoughts to return to his loyal wife. At the moment of his death they are once more brought together.

The American Dream

The American Dream is an ideal, shared by people who hope to make a success of their lives in America. The American Dream holds out the promise that through hard work people can overcome poverty and find a better future for themselves and their families.

Eddie's ambitions for Catherine can be seen in terms of the American Dream. He hopes that through her education she will be able to get a good job *someplace in New York in one of them nice buildings*. There is no reason to think that Eddie is not sincere in his aspirations for Catherine.

Marco and Rodolpho come to New York because they, too, share the American Dream. When Rodolpho proclaims '*I want to be an American*' he is saying that he wants something out of life and that America, unlike his own country, is able to provide an opportunity to achieve something. It is a sign of Rodolpho's intelligence that he knows it is only the employment opportunities that have brought him to America. Marco has left his own country because New York offers a chance for him to feed his family.

Part of the tragedy of the play is that the American Dream turns to dust. Eddie convinces himself that Rodolpho is using Catherine and as a result she will not be able to escape from the slum life of Red Hook. Eddie feels cheated because he worked so hard to support Catherine and to help her enjoy a better life and now he sees it being destroyed by Rodolpho. In reality, of course, it is Eddie himself who destroys the American Dream. It is Eddie who drives Marco to seek justice and revenge. Eddie's actions make a widow out of Beatrice and they shatter Catherine's innocence. Powerful feelings, those that attract Catherine to Eddie and those that compel Marco to seek justice, emerge in the play as stronger than any American Dream.

Social codes

This is an important theme in the play and it is linked to the idea of honour. *A View from the Bridge* is set in an Italian-American neighbourhood in New York and this society is seen to have its own code governing certain forms of behaviour. The play starts out with Alfieri pointing out that this is a community with a high regard for justice, *Justice is very important here*, even though the law may not always be observed. There is a clear sense that in this community justice is linked to the notion of honour. This sense of honour is both something very private and yet something that is publicly defined. The play ends with Eddie demanding justice from Marco for having slandered him: '*Wipin' the neighbourhood with my name like a dirty rag!*'

Eddie is deeply committed to the code of his society. He gets Beatrice to relate the story of what happened to Vinny Bolzano so that Catherine will understand the importance of secrecy. Eddie talks of helping his wife's cousins as an *honour*, something that he will be respected for in his society, and this is confirmed later when Louis says, '*Believe me, Eddie, you got a lotta credit comin' to you.*' Louis is not referring to credit in the financial sense but to the social credit that Eddie has gained by acting in a way of which society approves.

The society of Red Hook has a code of punishment as well as reward. This comes out in the story of Vinny and in Alfieri's dire warning to Eddie of the consequences of informing to the immigration authorities. The audience sees the consequences when Eddie tries to talk to his neighbours and friends after being accused by Marco. He has become a non-person and this robs Eddie of his identity as a member of that community. It is important to understand this because it explains why Eddie is so serious about standing his ground and meeting Marco. When his wife begs him to leave, Eddie asks '*Where?*' Faced with the wrath of his community Eddie is desperate to reclaim his name so that he can become someone once again. In the end, this need to regain the respect of his society is the most important thing in his life. (His concern with his 'name' has links with that of another Miller character – John Proctor in *The Crucible*.)

This idea of honour often overlaps with the notion of being a man in the macho sense of the word. Marco and Eddie both naturally assume that they must defend their honour by fighting. Rodolpho is different because he does not share this masculine need to accept violence and this is shown in the scene where he takes Eddie's hand and kisses it. When Eddie ignores this gesture and Beatrice asks '*Only blood is good?*' the answer, unfortunately, is yes. Eddie's response is revealing when he says, '*What he does don't mean nothin' to nobody!*' In this male world, honour is tied up with acting like a man and fighting to defend one's name.

We are told that Marco, before coming after Eddie, first goes to a church to pray, as if he is about to carry out some sacred duty. He sees himself as carrying out a punishment on behalf of his society. Although they face each other in fury, Eddie and Marco share the same basic values. They both accept the code of their society and they both believe in the importance of honour.

Thinking about the themes

? Based on the way some of the themes are explored in the play, fill in the three charts below with sets of rules.

The parental role	Rules for a good marriage	Red Hook's code of honour
Do	Do	Do
Don't	Don't	Don't

Now you know the rules, take a break before applying them.

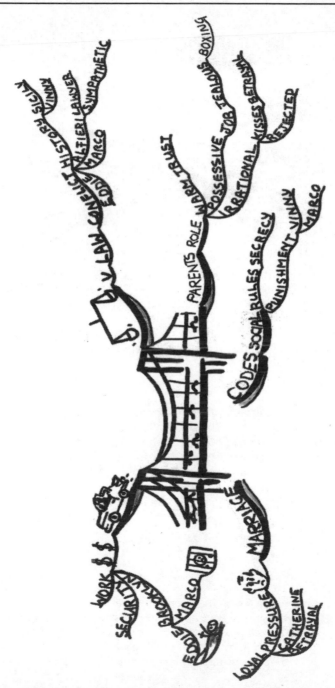

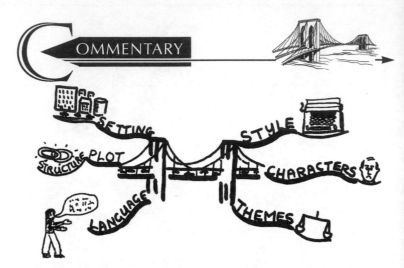

COMMENTARY

To help with revision, the Commentary breaks down the two Acts into a number of smaller scenes and begins with a list of key events or moments for each scene. This will remind you of key parts of the plot and help with last-minute revision. The Commentary itself comments on important moments in the section, bringing out aspects of the areas shown in the Mini Mind Map above.

ICONS

Whenever a particular theme is commented on, the icon for that theme appears in the margin (see p. xi for key). Also notice the 'Style and language' sections because being able to comment on the atmosphere, the dramatic mood and language used will help you to get an 'A' in your exam.

It will help you if you use the Commentary alongside the play itself. Read the pages from the play indicated at the beginning of each section – for example, (To p. 13, [*Alfieri walks into darkness*]) – and then read the Commentary. Or you may prefer to do it the other way around.

QUESTIONS

Remember that when a ✪ appears at the beginning of a question you should try to think about your answer before moving on to the next section. If the question puzzles you, discuss it with a friend or ask your teacher for help. And always **remember to take a short break** after each exercise.

Act 1

Entirely unromantic

(To p. 13, [*Alfieri walks into darkness*])

◆ Stage instructions set the scene.
◆ Alfieri reflects on the past and the present.
◆ Eddie is introduced.

Alfieri notices how the longshoremen's attitude towards him is affected by the fact that he is a lawyer. In Italy the law is regarded with mistrust and the immigrant longshoremen have brought this attitude with them to America. Justice is important but that does not always mean following the law. The tension that can develop between law and justice is an important theme that runs through *A View from the Bridge* and it is introduced at the beginning of the drama.

Alfieri talks of changes for the better and of how he no longer keeps a pistol in his filing cabinet. Nevertheless, we sense that Red Hook is a place where strict codes of behaviour are observed by the community. When he says, '*Justice is very important here*' he is talking about both the past and the present, and there is a sense that some things have not changed at all. The theme of law and justice overlaps with that of a social code because the Italian-American community is seen to have such a high regard for justice that it comes into conflict with the law. ✪ As an example of how important these themes are, remind yourself of the conversation in the prison where Alfieri and Catherine try to persuade Marco not to go after Eddie.

In this opening scene Alfieri is saying that, although justice is still important to the community, it is no longer obtained in the traditional way. The days of Al Capone, when disputes were settled with the help of machine guns, are a thing of the past. Now, says Alfieri, '*we settle for half, and I like it better.*' ✪ By thinking about how the play ends, can you see how ironic these words are?

STYLE AND LANGUAGE

Alfieri's choral role as someone who comments on what is happening by speaking directly to the audience is a feature of the play's style (see 'Who's who?', p. 14). His difference from the other characters also reveals itself in the way that he speaks. In his opening speech to the audience he talks of ancient history and of the differences between Sicily and New York. When he stops talking and we hear the language of ordinary longshoremen, it becomes obvious that his style of speaking is quite different from that of all the other characters in the play. Later in the play Alfieri becomes involved in the action and is a character in his own right and then he speaks in a more ordinary manner. ✪ Why do you think, just before Eddie is introduced, Alfieri pictures the scene of an ancient Roman lawyer listening to a case?

Eddie and Catherine

(From p. 13, when Eddie appears, to top of p. 15, *Her cousins landed*)
◆ Eddie returns home after a day's work.
◆ Eddie is concerned about Catherine's appearance and the way she attracts the attention of the opposite sex.

We are introduced to Eddie and his feelings of parental responsibility for Catherine. He reminds her of his promise to her mother and tells her she is still a baby. Notice Eddie's mixed feelings towards Catherine. At first he admires Catherine's appearance but then criticizes the way she attracts the attention of men. ✪ What advice does Eddie give Catherine? Do you think this is good advice?

STYLE AND LANGUAGE

The difference in the language style between Alfieri and everyone else in the play becomes apparent when this scene is compared with the opening scene of the play. *A View from the Bridge* started with Alfieri speaking in a very formal and stylized way. As an example, consider his language in the sentence where he describes the dock area of Red Hook: *This is the gullet of New York swallowing the tonnage of the world*. This is not the language of everyday, working-class people. He uses a **metaphor** because he wants to create an impression of Red Hook for the audience. Or, to take another example, consider how he first introduces Eddie. Instead of just stating plainly that Eddie works in a dockyard he places Eddie Carbone in a **context** by briefly creating in the audience's mind a sense of time and place: ...*Eddie Carbone, a longshoreman working the docks from Brooklyn Bridge to the breakwater where the open sea begins.*

Now compare this language with the opening dialogue between Eddie and Louis. The first words of Eddie are, '*Well, I'll see ya, fellas,*' and Louis replies '*You workin' tomorrow?*' Instead of writing 'you', we have *ya* and instead of 'working' we have *workin'*. Arthur Miller wants us to hear these characters speaking in a realistic manner. ✪ Write down what you might say if you met a friend from school in the street, and use a spelling that conveys the actual sound of your words.

Your task!

? Read the stage instructions at the beginning of the play once more and imagine the scene on the stage. Look at the sketch below and add any props that are missing. Mark in the area where most of the first conversation between Eddie and Catherine takes place.

Have a short break before Eddie arrives with important news.

News of Beatrice's cousins

(From p. 15 to bottom of p. 17, '*Go, Baby, set the table.*')

◆ Eddie has news that Beatrice's cousins have arrived earlier than expected in New York.

◆ The cousins are illegal immigrants from Italy.

◆ Eddie, after an initial concern, says they are welcome and Beatrice admires his attitude.

Beatrice is concerned about Eddie being able to cope with her cousins in their home. She looks into Eddie's eyes, saying that she is worried about him but cheers up when Eddie says it would be an honour to help her cousins. Beatrice seems a kind and sensible person. She admires Eddie for wanting to help fellow Italians arriving in America. At this stage in the play their marriage seems to be built on a solid foundation of trust and openness.

Eddie knows how poor Beatrice's cousins are and he remembers that his own father was once in a similar situation. America provides work and wages and this is at the heart of the American Dream. ❍ What does Eddie tell Beatrice is his reason for being a little concerned over the arrival of her cousins?

Catherine's new job

(Bottom of p. 17 to bottom of p. 19, [*Pause. Catherine lowers her eyes.*])

◆ Catherine has a chance to work in an office in the docks area.

◆ Eddie does not like the idea of Catherine working in the docks neighbourhood.

Notice how Catherine is anxious to win Eddie's approval. They are very close but we sense that Eddie might be possessive about Catherine. Notice how he twice interrupts Catherine at the top of page 17 and when Eddie asks about the job the stage instructions tell us that he is *strangely nervous*. This suggests that Eddie is a little alarmed at the prospect of Catherine going out to work. In the light of what will happen later in the play, we can sense that Eddie is uncomfortable with the idea that Catherine will be mixing with other men and meeting people.

Part of the American Dream is that opportunities are open to all and that anyone can succeed if prepared to work for it. A good education is seen by Eddie as a way for Catherine to escape her working-class neighbourhood and make something out of her life. *'So what did she go to school for?'* he says to Beatrice. ✪ What advice would you have given to Catherine?

A family dinner

(Bottom of p. 19 to halfway on p. 22, [*They continue eating in silence*].)

◆ Beatrice tells Eddie that the time has come for Catherine to leave school.
◆ Eddie accepts the situation but tells Catherine not to trust people.
◆ They eat dinner and joke about spiders.

Beatrice is in no doubt that Catherine should take the job. She has to spell out simple facts to Eddie to make him try to accept what is obviously true: *'I don't understand you; she's seventeen years old, you gonna keep her in the house all her life?'* Beatrice understands that a stage has been reached in their family where Catherine's independence needs to be accepted. We sense that Eddie is not convinced by his wife's logic. He distrusts people and the world that he knows, but when he relaxes with Catherine and Beatrice he seems happy.

Catherine becomes emotional once Eddie approves of her going to work. She wants his approval for this big step in her life. A stage instruction just before he agrees to her going out to work adds to our sense that Eddie, on the other hand, would prefer things to stay the same: [*with a sense of her childhood, her babyhood, and the years*]. ✪ What do you think Eddie means when he says, *'most people ain't people?'*

Notice the irony in Eddie's advice to Catherine. He tells her, *'don't trust nobody'* but an audience familiar with the plot knows that this applies to Eddie himself. At this stage Catherine trusts him completely, but this is all about to change.

Vinny – the boy who snitched

(Halfway on p. 22 to bottom of p. 25.)

◆ Eddie insists on absolute secrecy about the cousins moving into their home.

◆ Eddie tells Beatrice to tell Catherine the story of Vinny Bolzano.

◆ Eddie, in an emotional moment, wishes Catherine good luck.

◆ Beatrice and Eddie have a very brief conversation.

Eddie's advice about not saying a single word to anyone about the cousins shows him in the role of the protective father figure. Beatrice's comment – '*What do you mean? I understand*' – tells us that he is not saying anything Beatrice doesn't already know, but Eddie sees himself as the experienced male who can advise women about the ways of the world.

The story of Vinny reminds us of the theme introduced at the beginning of the play: justice is important but that does not always mean following the law. Vinny did what was right according to the law but it was not seen as the just thing to do. The attack on him by his own brothers and father is seen as a form of justice even though it was not lawful.

The story of Vinny also serves to illustrate the social code of society that operates in this community. Informing to the immigration authorities is seen as a crime against society and Beatrice says how *the whole neighbourhood was cryin*. The Red Hook community has its own strict rules about how people are expected to behave in certain situations.

Eddie fully understands this code of behaviour, '*You'll never see him no more, a guy do a thing like that? How's he gonna show his face?*' Vinny may not have been physically forced to leave the neighbourhood but he was effectively expelled by the community. ❖ Knowing that Eddie himself will do the same as Vinny, does it help to make us feel that he was acting out of character at that time? In his right mind, can you imagine Eddie informing on illegal immigrants from Italy?

While Catherine leaves the room to fetch his cigar, Eddie asks his wife why she is mad at him and Beatrice replies, '*I'm not mad. You're the one is mad.*' Eddie uses the word 'mad' in the sense of being annoyed but Beatrice uses it more in the sense of acting very strangely. Beatrice senses that Eddie is getting too emotional over the straightforward issue of Catherine going out to work. Try to remember this moment as a stage in the deteriorating relationship between Eddie and Beatrice. ❂ Should Beatrice be more direct with her husband concerning the need to accept Catherine's right to now make her own decisions?

STYLE AND LANGUAGE

Notice how the dramatic mood changes towards the end of this section. After the story of Vinny, Eddie continues to play the role of the experienced man by giving more advice to Catherine and explaining the process of illegal immigration but then the stage instructions indicate a change in the atmosphere. We are told, at the top of p. 25, that tears come to his eyes. Catherine is not sure how to respond to Eddie here – we are told she is embarrassed and that she tries to laugh – and Eddie himself reaches for a cigar as if to comfort himself. The prospect of Catherine going out into the world is an emotional moment for Eddie. He knows that Catherine as a working adult will no longer be the baby in the family that he has supported and protected. This is something that Eddie finds difficult to accept. He would prefer things to stay the same.

Try talking to yourself!

?   Read aloud to yourself the lines spoken by Eddie from the bottom of page 24, '*So you gonna start Monday, heh, Madonna?*', to just before Catherine goes to fetch his cigar, '*I left a cigar in my other coat, I think.*' Imagine you are talking to Catherine and practise pausing between the lines, as if you were an actor preparing for the part. How do you think Eddie is making Catherine and Beatrice feel?

?   Read the following lines aloud to yourself. If necessary look them up in the play and identify the

speaker. Try to say the lines in the way you imagine
the character speaking. Also, ask yourself what the
lines tell us about a character or a theme in the play.
Then fill in the chart.

1 *'Oh, there were many here who were justly shot by
   unjust men.'*
2 *'Now, don't aggravate me, Katie, you are walkin' wavy.'*
3 *'Look, you gotta ger used to it, she's no baby no more.'*
4 *'Just remember, kid, you can quicker get back a
   million dollars that was stole than a word that you
   gave away.'*
5 *'I'm not mad ....You're the one is mad.'*

Quote 1 is spoken by _____ and it illustrates an
aspect of the _____ theme.

_____ utters quote 2 and it is an early indication of
the way he takes his role too seriously.

In quote 3 _____ speaks to _____ in an attempt to
remind him of the limits of his parental role.

Quote 4 is an aspect of the _____ theme and later
in the play these words will apply to _____ himself.
These words are spoken by _____ and they are
closer to the truth than _____ realizes.

---

*Now have a break before there is a knock on
the door.*

The cousins arrive

(Bottom of p. 25 to middle of p. 31 [*He helps* BEATRICE *set out
the coffee things*].)

◆ Alfieri announces the arrival of Marco and Rodolpho.
◆ The cousins talk about the hard times back in Italy.
◆ Marco plans to eventually return to Italy and his wife and family.
◆ Rodolpho talks of becoming an American and returning to
   Italy to buy a motorcycle.

Marco is overome with emotion at the thought of being able to send money back to his family and Rodolpho describes how hard it is to find work in Italy. Their conversation helps us realize the persuasive power of the American Dream. America will fulfil their dreams: money for Marco's family and a motorcycle for Rodolpho that will make him someone back in Italy.

In Rodolpho's story about owning a motorcycle he says, *'But a man who rides up on a great machine, this man is responsible, this man exists.'* ✪ Do you think Rodolpho is being foolish in thinking a motorcycle would transform his life or has he hit on a sensible idea that could prove successful back in Italy? Rodolpho feels that he will gain social recognition, and employment, when he has a motorcycle. He will be someone because society will judge him to have some status. The power of the community is strong and being seen to be someone is important. This will become very clear later in the play when Eddie knows he has lost the respect of his community.

✪ How does this scene suggest that Catherine might be attracted to Rodolpho? Imagine you are the director and giving advice to the actors about how best to convey this growing attraction between them. ✪ What advice would you give?

STYLE AND LANGUAGE

By speaking the words aloud, listen to the tone of Alfieri's words as the stage lights go down on Eddie sitting in his armchair and come up on Alfieri himself. This is not everyday, ordinary language. Alfieri is standing back from Eddie, summarizing his life and telling the story almost as if it had to happen in the way it did. This is an aspect of his choral role as a commentator on the unfolding drama. If we know how the story ends then the last sentence, in particular, sounds a little fearful and ominous.

Rodolpho sings and Eddie stops him

(Middle of p. 31 to top of p. 34.)

◆ Rodolpho tells how he once substituted for a professional singer who was ill.

◆ Catherine invites him to sing 'Paper Doll'.

◆ Eddie interrupts Rodolpho on the grounds that possible informers might realize there are strangers in the apartment.

◆ Eddie disapproves of Catherine wearing high heels and she changes into flat shoes.

◆ As Catherine is putting sugar in Rodolpho's coffee, the lights go up on Alfieri who speaks of trouble lying ahead.

In this scene we see that Eddie is uncomfortable with Rodolpho's presence and we sense that this is due to Eddie's awareness of the growing attraction between Rodolpho and Catherine. For the first time we see Catherine getting annoyed at Eddie's attitude and this is made clear by the stage instructions: [*Embarrassed now, angered,* CATHERINE *goes out into the bedroom.*] ✪ Does Eddie interrupt Rodolpho singing simply because it might arouse suspicion? Could the words of the songs be seen as a comment on Eddie's own feelings for Catherine?

The stage instructions also tell us that Beatrice gets up from the table and gives Eddie *a cold look*. She realizes that her husband is acting unreasonably and wants him to know that she disapproves.

 ### STYLE AND LANGUAGE

Look again at the various stage instructions at the end of this scene (bottom of p. 33). The stage lights go down as Eddie is looking worried as he watches Rodolpho and Catherine sharing a private moment. Then the lights focus on Alfieri as he speaks of trouble looming ahead for Eddie. Is seems clear that this will involve Catherine and Rodolpho.

Notice also how the Alfieri's language here is similar in style to his earlier remarks at the top of page 26.

Characters discuss Rodolpho

(Top of p. 34 to middle of p. 38 [... *CATHERINE stops him at the door*].)

◆ Three weeks have passed and Eddie is on edge, waiting for Catherine to return from the cinema with Rodolpho.

◆ Eddie tells Beatrice that he doesn't like Rodolpho.

◆ Beatrice asks her husband why he hasn't made love to her for three months.

◆ Eddie listens to Mike and Louis talking about how popular Rodolpho is.

Eddie is clearly unhappy with the close relationship developing between Rodolpho and Catherine. He accuses Rodolpho of being effeminate, meaning that he acts more like a woman than a 'real' man, by suspecting that his blond hair is not natural and that his singing at work makes him more *like a chorus girl*. He accuses Rodolpho of using Catherine, *'B., he's taking her for a ride!'*

❂ Is Eddie jealous of Rodolpho because he himself is attracted to Catherine in a way that he cannot admit? Or is he genuinely concerned for her welfare? Not all questions have a simple yes or a no answer; maybe Eddie is jealous and caring at the same time.

This conversation between Beatrice and Eddie tells us a lot about Beatrice. She is observant and understands that Eddie is acting strangely. She tries to make Eddie see sense and when, for example, he questions whether Rodolpho's hair is really blond she points out that he knows another blond person. When this has no effect she is more direct and insistent, *'Listen, you ain't gonna start nothin' here.'* She goes on to confront him with the fact that he is neglecting their own sexual relationship: *'When am I gonna be a wife again, Eddie?'*

Beatrice has more straight talking. She spells out the simple fact that Catherine and Rodolpho must be allowed to develop in their own way, even if this means making mistakes: *'What're you gonna stand over her till she's forty?'*

STYLE AND LANGUAGE

What is the dramatic function of the scene where Louis and Mike tell Eddie how likeable and popular Rodolpho is amongst his fellow longshoremen? Exam questions that ask about the dramatic function or the dramatic purpose of a scene are common. Such a question is asking how the scene contributes to our understanding of the play as a whole. It is also often asking you to relate the scene to what has gone before and/or what is about to happen. The following points could all be part of your answer to the question:

- When Louis says *'Believe me, Eddie, you got a lotta credit comin' to you,'* we are reminded of the social code theme. Louis and Mike are not individual characters in this play but together they represent the voice of the community and the opinion of the community is an important factor in this play. Through their comments the audience learns that the community has noted and warmly approved of Eddie's behaviour in taking in the two illegal immigrants.

- The words of Louis are also full of **dramatic irony** because later events will reveal the exact opposite of this. The community will condemn Eddie when he informs on the cousins.

- We learn for the first time that Marco is a very strong man. This will become significant later on in the play when Eddie and Marco fight.

- The audience is inclined to believe Louis and Mike when they talk of Rodolpho's good sense of humour and his lively character that cheers people up. It helps us understand why Catherine falls in love with him. It also makes clearer the difference between Marco's character and Rodolpho's.

- The audience sees that Eddie is acting unreasonably when he questions Rodolpho's personality and his motives for being with Catherine. If other people enjoy Rodolpho's company then why is Eddie always so negative about him? In the very next scene Catherine will be shocked by Eddie's account of what Rodolpho wants.

- We see Louis and Mike reinforcing the truth of what Beatrice said earlier to Eddie: *'He's a nice kid, what do you want from him?'*

Eddie confronts Catherine

(Middle of p. 38 to top of p. 42, 'Katie!')

◆ When Catherine and Rodolpho return from the cinema Eddie wants to speak to Catherine alone.
◆ Catherine tells Eddie that she likes Rodolpho.
◆ Eddie tells Catherine that Rodolpho wants to marry her only so that he can become an American citizen.
◆ Catherine is very upset and tearfully tells Eddie that he has the wrong opinion of Rodolpho.

There will be others but this is the first climax in the relationship between Catherine and Eddie. Catherine, like Beatrice, cannot understand what he has against Rodolpho: 'He blesses you, and you don't talk to him hardly.' At this stage it is clear that she is unaware of his possessiveness and his jealousy of Rodolpho. When he asks a direct question, 'You like him, Katie?', she does not, however, flinch from telling him what she honestly feels: 'Yeah. I like him.' This is an important moment in their relationship. In her own way she is asserting her independence and Eddie is not happy with this. He goes on to accuse Rodolpho of using her.

When Eddie does accuse Rodolpho of using Catherine she is genuinely surprised that he should think this. Coming as it does straight after the scene where Louis and Mike speak so warmly of him, it is difficult not to agree with Catherine that, 'You got him all wrong, Eddie.' However, such is the trust that Catherine has for Eddie, she is upset by his accusations. The stage instructions tell us that she is *pained*. Look ahead to the first scene of Act 2. ❂ Can you see how there Catherine is remembering the conversation she is having here with Eddie about Rodolpho's motives?

Now try these exercises

?   In this scene Catherine experiences a range of conflicting emotions. Draw a graph showing how her feelings change between first seeing Eddie at the door and breaking down in tears as she enters the house. Number each high or low point and give a word that describes how she feels at that moment. Show your graph to your teacher to see if he or she agrees with your interpretation.

? For each number on the graph give a line from the scene that acts as support for the word you used to describe how she felt.

? For each of the lines below, spoken by or about Rodolpho, say what you think it tells us about Rodolpho's character. It may help if you look up the line and consider the context (this means look at the dialogue before and after the actual quote and consider the situation in which they occur).

'With a motorbike in Italy you will never starve any more.'

'Well, he's a kid; he don't know how to behave himself yet.'

'You take one look at him – everybody's happy.'

'I would like to go to Broadway once, Eddie.'

? When Rodolpho leaves Catherine and Eddie he goes for a walk by the river. What do you think goes through his mind as he walks?

Have a break before considering another emotional conversation.

Women's talk

(Top of p. 42 to just before the lights focus on Alfieri at the top of p. 45.)

◆ Beatrice tells Eddie to leave Catherine alone and he walks out of the house.

◆ Beatrice and Catherine discuss how best to deal with Eddie.

◆ Beatrice tells Catherine she is a woman now and must act accordingly.

◆ Catherine agrees with Beatrice that it is time to make Eddie see sense.

At the beginning of this scene, when Beatrice says '*You going to leave her alone? Or you gonna drive me crazy?*', a crisis is developing between her and her husband. Beatrice knows that her husband is overreacting to Rodolpho and she wants to try to sort things out for the best. She calls to Catherine who is about to go into her bedroom, '*Listen, Catherine.*' [CATHERINE *halts, turns to her sheepishly.*], because she wants to try to regain a meaningful relationship with her husband. Beatrice knows that emotionally Eddie has become too close to Catherine for everyone's good.

It is Beatrice who spells out for Catherine what Catherine herself is now realizing. Eddie is not acting reasonably because he is possessive about Catherine. He does not want her to marry anyone because then she will no longer belong to him. It is not stated directly but there is a clear sense that Eddie is attracted to Catherine because she is a woman and not simply because he feels protective towards her as a stepdaughter.

Beatrice's advice to Catherine about behaving towards Eddie as an independent woman and not like a child is sensible. Eddie has grown too close to Catherine and having Catherine walk around the house in her slip does not help matters. It is time for Catherine to distance herself from Eddie because the relationship has become an unhealthy one. Look ahead to p. 81 where Beatrice tries to defend Eddie by saying that Catherine and herself also have some responsibility for what has happened to Eddie. ❂ Do you think this is the sort of thing Beatrice had in mind when she said this to Catherine?

This scene ends with Catherine's realization that Beatrice is right. Look again at the final stage instructions. This is an important moment for Catherine because she knows what Beatrice is saying and she has made a decision.

STYLE AND LANGUAGE

When reading the bare words of a play it helps a lot to imagine how they are spoken by the character. At the end of this scene, when Beatrice says it is time for Catherine to distance herself from Eddie, this is the dialogue without the stage instructions:

CATHERINE: All right ... if I can.
BEATRICE: Honey ... you gotta.
CATHERINE: Okay.

Imagine Beatrice has just asked for the price of a bus fare because she has no change but she is in a hurry. If this was the context then the lines would be spoken in a certain kind of way. Read the lines aloud as if Beatrice has just asked for money for a bus fare. Now consider the actual context in which Beatrice is really speaking and read the stage instructions. Read the lines again, bearing in mind all you know about Beatrice and Catherine and Eddie. ❷ Do you notice the important difference?

Men's talk

(Top of p. 45 to when the stage lights go out on Alfieri on p. 50.)
◆ Eddie visits Alfieri to see if the law can be used against Rodolpho.
◆ The lawyer explains that this is a private matter where the law does not apply.
◆ Eddie explains to Alfieri that he thinks Rodolpho is homosexual and more like a woman than a 'real' man.
◆ The lawyer advises Eddie to draw back from Catherine and let her get on with her own life.
◆ Alfieri senses the tragedy that is looming ahead.

Eddie has convinced himself that Rodolpho is only using Catherine and he hopes that the law can do something about it. Alfieri explains that the law cannot tell people how to feel, but to Eddie this is a case of obvious injustice and he expects the law to be able to help.

Being a lawyer, Alfieri obviously represents the law, but he does not simply represent the law in a narrow, mechanical sense. He has a regard for the community and is upset at the thought that Eddie is heading for trouble. He even consults *a very wise old woman* about the situation. Alfieri says that the wise old woman *only nodded, and said, 'Pray for him...'*
❷ What do you think might be suggested by her nodding and her suggestion that a prayer be said for him?

Notice that Alfieri has now become a character in the play. He has told Eddie there is nothing the law can do about the relationship between Rodolpho and Catherine. He also reminds Eddie that the law would only be interested in the fact that he is an illegal immigrant. Alfieri is now playing his part in the unfolding drama although he continues in the role of someone able to comment on the action as a whole.

 Rodolpho's sexuality is questioned by Eddie but it tells us more about Eddie's possessiveness towards Catherine than about Rodolpho himself. Instead of being able to see that Rodolpho has the skill to alter a dress, Eddie uses it as an example of his femininity and unsuitability as a husband. Eddie's accusation against Rodolpho – *'He's stealing from me!'* – brings out his possessiveness. He is hurt by the fact that Catherine prefers Rodolpho to someone like himself who has struggled and worked hard to provide for Catherine.

Alfieri tries to give sensible advice when he says, *'She wants to get married, Eddie. She can't marry you, can she?'*, but Eddie's reaction is one of strong fury. Alfieri, accidentally it seems, has touched on the possibility that Eddie's feelings towards Catherine are more than just those of a caring father-figure. The lawyer seems to have touched a raw nerve and Eddie is very uncomfortable with this.

STYLE AND LANGUAGE

The style of the language changes once again when Alfieri speaks. His words are directed to the audience and the past tense – *'And so I – waited here'* – reminds us that the play is unfolding events that have already happened. ✪ If you can remember reading the play for the first time can you recall what you thought was going to happen when Alfieri said *'I knew where he was going to end?'* When reading the play for the first time another line of Alfieri's creates dramatic tension because the audience may suspect but cannot know for sure what is meant by, *'I could see every step coming, step after step, like a dark figure walking down a hall towards a certain door.'*

Test yourself

? One example of dramatic irony has already been given (p. 38) and there are two more in the lines below. Identify the speaker and remind yourself why they carry a sense of dramatic irony.

'His eyes were like tunnels; my first thought was that he had committed a crime.'

'Oh, Jesus, no, I wouldn't do nothin' about that, I mean –'

? There is a similarity between the advice that Alfieri gives to Eddie in this scene and the advice that Beatrice gave to Catherine in the scene before. Find a line spoken by Beatrice and put it alongside a line from Alfieri that says more or less the same thing.

? The following lines are worth memorizing because they tell us something interesting about a character. Fill in the missing words and try to learn them by heart.

'The guy ain't _____ .'

'But sometimes ... there's too much. You know? There's too much and it goes _____ .'

'... puts his dirty filthy hands on like a goddam _____ .'

? Alfieri speaks of a passion that had moved into his body, like a stranger. Does this make you feel a little sorry for Eddie, as if he cannot control what is happening to him? Whether you feel sorry for him or not, try to give a reason for your opinion.

Take a break before tackling the dramatic conclusion to Act 1.

An after-dinner talk

(From p. 50 to p. 54 when Catherine puts a record on.)

◆ Eddie, Beatrice, Rodolpho and Marco engage in small talk after dinner.

◆ The mood changes when Eddie criticizes Rodolpho.

When Eddie makes a joke about women in Italy having affairs with other men while their husbands are working in America both Marco and Rodolpho make clear that this does not happen very often. *'Very few surprises'* says Marco, and Rodolpho adds that *'It's more strict in our town.'* The power of the community, the code of society, is felt to be very strong in Italy. This gives Eddie an excuse to start criticizing Rodolpho by pointing out that there are also strict rules in the Italian community in New York.

From the way that Eddie criticizes Rodolpho it seems clear that he has not taken on board the advice of either his wife or Alfieri. He does not seem prepared to let Catherine go, despite Rodolpho's willingness to listen to him: *'I have respect for her, Eddie. I do anything wrong?'* Marco is also careful about trying to make sure there is no misunderstanding. He tells Rodolpho not to keep Catherine out late. However, Eddie seems determined to make his point yet again and, at the top of p. 50, the stage instructions indicate that he is angry.

At the start of this scene there is a sense of domestic harmony as everyone engages in small talk. As this mood collapses, Beatrice tries to restore it and keep the peace. She defends Rodolpho against her husband's hint that he has dragged Catherine away without permission. She goes on to tell Eddie to act like an uncle and not a father. She wants Eddie to leave Catherine alone so that her own relationship with Eddie can continue as it once was.

(From p. 51 when Catherine puts on a record to the end of Act 1.)

A battle of wills

◆ Catherine puts on a record and asks Rodolpho to dance with her.
◆ Eddie says that if he had Rodolpho's talents he would work in a dress store.
◆ Eddie gives Rodolpho a boxing lesson.
◆ In a trial of strength over the lifting of a chair Marco is triumphantly the stronger of the two men.

Eddie has not taken to heart the advice of his wife and Alfieri, but Catherine seems to have remembered Beatrice's advice to distance herself from Eddie. It is her decision alone to ask Rodolpho for a dance and the stage instruction describes her as being *flushed with revolt*. She is making it clear that her relationship with Rodolpho will continue, whatever Eddie might think. This is a clear example of her developing sense of independence and it causes Eddie to feel uneasy.

Beatrice acts again to try to keep peace in the house. At first she thinks the boxing lesson is harmless fun but then she realizes Eddie is trying to teach Rodolpho a very different kind of lesson. ✪ Identify the stage instruction that makes it clear Beatrice is alarmed by Eddie's behaviour and wants to make sure it goes no further.

STYLE AND LANGUAGE

The last scene of Act 1 is very dramatic to read and even more so when it is acted out on the stage. It is always worth remembering that *A View from the Bridge* is a play, written to be performed, and that the meaning comes from what the characters do on the stage as well as what they say.

When Catherine invites Rodolpho to dance with her she is asserting her independence and signalling to Eddie that he cannot control her life. An audience, seeing her take his hand for a dance, understands its dramatic function.

When Eddie offers Rodolpho a boxing lesson the audience is probably suspicious of his motives. When Rodolpho staggers from Eddie's blow the audience realizes this was not an accidental punch. He is delivering a warning to Rodolpho.

Marco, however, is quick to respond and when he lifts the chair above Eddie's head the audience also realizes that he will not let his brother be bullied by Eddie. Marco says only one word, '*Here*,' and this by itself does not communicate much to the audience. The stage instructions, on the other hand, take up two paragraphs and the last sentence has more than 50 words. The playwright wants anyone performing or reading the play to understand the dramatic function of

Marco's act. It is dramatically effective – meaning that what happens on the stage is successfully communicated to the audience – and yet hardly a word is spoken. At the end of Act 1 we are very aware of the growing tension between Eddie and his wife's cousins.

Now try this

? There are various details in this scene that add to its dramatic success. Each of the following questions focuses on a detail and asks about how it adds to our understanding of a character or a theme in the play.
  - Why do you think Catherine chose 'Paper Doll' as the record to dance to?
  - Why does Beatrice inform Eddie that Rodolpho and Catherine have bought only three records?
  - When Catherine first asked Rodolpho to dance he tried to give an excuse not to. Yet after the boxing lesson he takes the initiative and asks Catherine to dance. What do you think this might indicate?

? The stage instructions in the last scene of Act 1 also add to our understanding of the characters. For each of the following say briefly what it tells us about the character at this moment in the drama:
  'You wanna dance, Rodolpho?' [EDDIE freezes.]
  'That's why the water-front is no place for him.' [They stop dancing. RODOLPHO turns off phonegraph.]
  [He has been unconsciously twisting the newspaper into a tight roll.]
  'No, no he didn't hurt me.' [To EDDIE with a certain gleam and a smile] *'I was only surprised.'*

LOOKING BACK ON ACT 1

? Draw a line from each statement opposite to one of the themes below. Some themes might have more than one line going to them and one of the statements could be connected to two of the themes. It does not matter how messy the page looks when you have finished because, for this exercise, the process of linking the statements to themes is more important than neatness.

- At the beginning of the play Alfieri talks about how the longshoremen are a little uneasy in his presence and how in the past men were shot down on the streets.

- Before Louis and Rodolpho arrive, Eddie tells Beatrice to relate the story of what happened to Vinny.

- Eddie, in an emotional state after wishing Catherine good luck in her new job, asks Beatrice why she is annoyed and she replies, '*I'm not mad. You're the one is mad.*'

- On the night he arrives, Rodolpho says he wants to be an American.

- The song 'Paper Doll' includes the line *And it's tough to love a doll that's not your own.*

- On the night that Rodolpho and Catherine go to the cinema Beatrice asks her husband, '*When am I gonna be a wife again, Eddie?*'

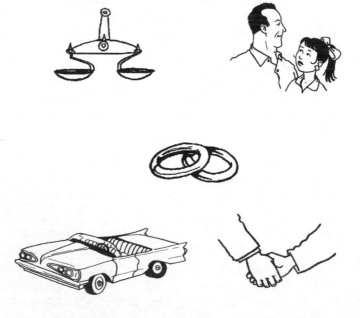

? The following list covers nine main episodes in Act 1 but they are not in the correct order. Try re-ordering them without looking at the play and then check your answer. Make any necessary corrections so that you end up with a list in the correct order.

- Marco and Rodolpho arrive.
- Alfieri sets the scene.
- Dinner with Eddie, Beatrice and Catherine.
- Discussion between Beatrice and Eddie about Rodolpho and Catherine.
- Beatrice talks to Catherine about the need for her to be more independent.
- Louis and Mike talk with Eddie.
- Conversation between Eddie and Catherine after she returns from the cinema.
- Chair-lifting contest after Eddie, Beatrice, Catherine, Marco and Rodolpho have dinner together.
- Alfieri is visited by Eddie.

A possible mnemonic for the correct sequence could be: A Diner Might Discuss Long Conversations Before Dessert Comes.

It's interval time – have a rest before resuming your seat.

Act 2

Catherine and Rodolpho discuss their future

(From the beginning of Act 2 to just before Eddie arrives back home, p. 63.)

- ◆ Rodolpho and Catherine are alone together in the house.
- ◆ Catherine asks about the two of them going to live in Italy.
- ◆ Rodolpho wants to stay in America where there is work.
- ◆ They discuss how best to deal with Eddie.

The opening scene of Act 2 makes it clear that the relationship between Catherine and Rodolpho is a strong and loving one. They are honest with each other and discuss their feelings and fears in an open and trusting way. Even though Beatrice and Eddie are not present, their relationship can be compared with the relationship between Catherine and Rodolpho. Look back to the scene where Beatrice talks to Eddie outside their house, on the night Catherine has gone to the cinema with Rodolpho, and compare the way the two couples talk to one another. ○ How does Rodolpho treat Catherine compared with the way Eddie treats his wife?

Eddie is not present but the relationship between him and Catherine is at the heart of this scene. Catherine is asking about going to live in Italy because she sees it as a way of repairing the damage done to her relationship with Eddie. She thinks that if she could make Eddie see that Rodolpho is not just using her then all Eddie's anger and resentment would go away. ○ Do you think this would work? Would Eddie be content if he knew Rodolpho really does love Catherine?

We learn more about Catherine in this scene. She is now very aware of how unhappy Eddie is and she wants to restore the mutual warmth that once characterized their life together. Rodolpho is sympathetic and understanding but he points out that, nevertheless, she must separate from Eddie if he cannot accept the love they have for each other.

We also learn more about Rodolpho from this scene. In earlier scenes it was possible to think he was a little naive, an unsophisticated young man from Italy who knew little of the ways of the world, and too easily impressed by the bright lights of Broadway. In this scene the audience realizes that he is more aware of what America has to offer: '*I want to be an American so I can work, that is the only wonder here – work!*' Just before this, also speaking of America, he sarcastically asks '*It's so wonderful?*' Rodolpho is not taken in by the American Dream and it is only the lack of work back in Italy that keeps him in New York.

STYLE AND LANGUAGE

Rodolpho is an interesting character. We know that he can cook, sing and make dresses and his sense of humour endears him to others. His interesting character is also reflected in his language. When, for example, he is trying to tell Catherine that it would be unfair to bring her back to a life of poverty in Italy he says, '*I would be a criminal stealing your face. In two years you would have an old, hungry face.*' When trying to convince her of Eddie's responsibility to let her conduct her own life, he tells a little story about the injustice of preventing a bird from flying. It is an effective comparison. ❖ Try to find another example, either in this scene or an earlier one, of Rodolpho's imaginative use of language.

Confrontation time

(From Eddie's appearance on p. 63 to when he leaves the apartment, in the middle of p. 65.)

◆ Eddie arrives home drunk, having finished early for Christmas.

◆ Eddie tells Rodolpho to leave and Catherine says she will also leave.

◆ Eddie forces a kiss on Catherine and provokes Rodolpho into attacking him.

◆ Eddie then kisses Rodolpho and warns him to leave the apartment.

When Eddie tells Rodolpho to '*Get your stuff and get outa here,*' Catherine has no hesitation about choosing to go with him. However, although the decision is not difficult to make, it causes her great distress and this is made clear by the stage instruction: [*Her sobs of pity and love for him break her composure.*] From her conversation with Rodolpho before Eddie arrived we know that she feels very unhappy about turning her back on him. She has so many pleasant memories of Eddie from her childhood that it is painful having to separate from him under unhappy circumstances. Even at this stage she earnestly hopes for a change of heart on his part and the stage directions tell us that she [*clasps her hands prayerfully*] when pleading, '*Oh, Eddie, don't be like that!*'

The scene ends with Catherine tearing at his face in her desperation to protect Rodolpho. It is a very painful moment both for her and for Eddie. He is left standing in the room in tears and they both now know that things will never again be the same between them.

 STYLE AND LANGUAGE

This scene is a highly charged one and, like the scene that brings Act 1 to a conclusion, it is dramatically very successful. Eddie's act of kissing Catherine dramatizes openly what the audience has long suspected. His feelings for Catherine are far more than those of a caring father-figure and under the influence of drink he shows what he really feels. As Rodolpho tries to stop him he says, '*Stop that! Have respect for her!*' This is ironic because Eddie has been unfairly accusing Rodolpho of showing a lack of respect for Catherine when really this is something he lacks himself.

Even more dramatic is the kissing of Rodolpho by Eddie. It is possible to imagine Eddie justifying this by claiming he wanted to expose Rodolpho's effeminate nature. Really, however, it seems to say far more about Eddie's own confused sexual feelings. It is important to try to understand the two kisses as dramatic acts that communicate Eddie's confused feelings to the audience without the need for words. Like Marco's lifting of the chair at the end of Act 1, the kisses perform a dramatic function.

Take a break before some exercises.

Some exercises to try

? Match the numbers below with the correct letters.

1 *'And tell him also, and tell yourself, please, that I am not a beggar and you are not a horse, a gift, a favour for a poor immigrant.'*
2 *'I would – just feel ashamed if I made him sad.'*
3 *'Come on, show me! What're you gonna be? Show me!'*
4 *'Watch your step, submarine. By rights they oughta throw you back in the water.'*
5 *'There's nothing! Nothing, nothing, nothing!'*

A At this stage in the play Catherine finds it very painful to turn her back on Eddie.
B Rodolpho is no fool, he has a sense of dignity and self-respect.
C There is a nasty side to Eddie's character and he knows how to hurt people's feelings.
D Terrible poverty in Italy made people like Louis and Rodolpho emigrate illegally to America.
E Dramatic tension is created when the audience feels Eddie might betray Rodolpho to the immigration authorities.

? The line below ranges from the negative extreme of being hateful and despicable to the positive extreme of being saintly and kind. Put a capital E in a position that best represents how you feel about Eddie at this stage in the play. If you think he is totally hateful the E will go very close to the left side but if you are unsure how you feel about him the E might go somewhere around the middle. Do the same with the letter C for Catherine and the letter R for Rodolpho. When you have finished show your results to your teacher to see if he or she agrees with you.

Hateful and _____Warm-hearted and
despicable   kind

? Mark these statements as either True or False.
1 Rodolpho is sensitive to changes in Catherine's moods.

2 Eddie has been spending all his money on drink.
3 Catherine has taken Beatrice's advice and now thinks of herself as an independent woman.
4 Catherine is horrified at the way Eddie behaves when he returns home drunk.
5 Eddie refuses to leave the apartment until Rodolpho leaves first.

Answers to the exercises above

1 = B; 2 = A; 3 = C; 4 = E; 5 = D.
In the second exercise try to find a line from the first two scenes of Act 2 that supports each answer.
1 True; 2 False; 3 True; 4 True; 5 False.

Eddie makes the phone call

(From middle of p. 65 to p. 67 where Eddie makes the phone call.)

◆ It is 27 December and Eddie returns to see Alfieri.
◆ Alfieri is worried about Eddie but has to tell him that the law is not on his side.
◆ Eddie makes a phone call to the Immigration Bureau and informs on his wife's cousins.

Alfieri's description of Eddie – '*But I will never forget how dark the room became when he looked at me; his eyes were like tunnels*' – suggests that Eddie is now obsessed with trying to separate Catherine and Rodolpho. His relationship with Catherine has broken down but he will not admit this to himself. He desperately hopes that Alfieri, as a lawyer, will be able to do something. It seems as if he is hoping that if only Rodolpho was out of the way then the relationship between himself and Catherine would return to the way it once was.

Eddie has convinced himself that Rodolpho's sexuality is suspect and that therefore he has a good reason for wishing to prevent their marriage. He tells the lawyer that he provoked Rodolpho into attacking him in order to show Catherine that he was not a 'real' man. Notice that Eddie does not tell Alfieri about kissing Catherine or Rodolpho. The story that he gives to the lawyer is a selective one and perhaps he has even blocked out from his own mind the kisses he forced on Catherine and Rodolpho. Instead of telling Alfieri the whole truth he mentions how Catherine's mother *will turn over in the grave*. Again, it seems as if he is giving himself an excuse for feeling so aggressive towards Rodolpho. The audience, on the other hand, suspects that Eddie is lying to himself about his real feelings for Catherine and he will not admit to himself that there is a sexual aspect to his emotional state of mind. ✪ Why do you think Alfieri says that he kept wanting to call the police but *nothing had happened*?

Alfieri gives his own views on the relationship between justice and the law. He says how *the law is nature* and goes on to explain what he means by this: '*The law is only a word for what has a right to happen.*' Alfieri believes that what is just – which is another way of saying *what has a right to happen* – and what is lawful is, or should be, the same thing. ✪ Can you think of a law that exists in your country that you would say is unjust? If not, can you think of a law that existed in your country in the past that you think was unjust?

Alfieri might well agree with the example you thought of when responding to this question. The lawyer is not so foolish as to think that every law is a just one. He explains this by saying, '*When the law is wrong it's because it's unnatural.*' So for Alfieri, when the law is doing its job it reflects natural justice, what has a right to happen. When the law is not doing its job properly, according to Alfieri, this is because it is going against natural justice. ✪ What do you think? Would you agree with Alfieri? When you thought of an example of a law that was unjust was this because you thought something has, or had, a right to happen – whatever the law might say?

Alfieri knows that Eddie is thinking of making a phone call to the Immigration Bureau. He warns him not to do this and the reason he gives is an interesting one: '*You won't have a friend in the world.*' The lawyer knows that if Eddie informs on his wife's cousins he will not be forgiven by the community. He will have broken a law that the community has made for itself and there will be a price to pay. The code of society, or at least the code of Italian society in America at this time, will punish him socially by turning their backs on him and treating him like an outcast.

What is interesting is that by phoning the Immigration Bureau Eddie will be following the law. You might think that Alfieri, as a lawyer, would not have a problem with this. It would seem that he regards this law as an unjust one. It is worth remembering that Alfieri knows full well that Louis and Rodolpho are illegal immigrants but he never thinks of informing the authorities. Quite the opposite, for he warns Eddie not to do this. Or does Alfieri see a conflict between the law on the one hand, even a just law, and the code of a society that is stronger than the law?

 The lawyer asks Eddie about his wife's opinion of what has happened. Both the stage instructions and Eddie's reply are revealing: [*unwilling to pursue this*]: '*Nobody's talking much in the house.*' Eddie is unwilling to pursue the matter of Beatrice's opinion because he knows that she does not agree with him. He may well be right when he says nobody is saying much because it is not difficult to imagine that the atmosphere in the apartment is very strained and uncomfortable. However, it is also possible to imagine that Beatrice has spoken her mind and told her husband exactly what she thinks about it. ✪ Do you think Beatrice has kept her feelings and opinions to herself or do you think she has already spoken to her husband? Before responding to this question, think about the kind of person Beatrice is and whether she is the kind of person to keep silent about what has taken place.

STYLE AND LANGUAGE

It has been noticed earlier how Alfieri's language is different from ordinary, everyday language. Look back to page 35 in this book where it was noted how Alfieri speaks about events as if they had to happen, as if they were inevitable. At the beginning of this scene we once again hear Alfieri speaking about Eddie and the unfolding events in a strange way: '*...when I saw him walking through my doorway, I knew why I had waited. And if I seem to tell this like a dream, it was that way.*'

He goes on to talk about feeling *transfixed*, a word that means 'unable to move', meaning that he feels powerless to prevent what is about to happen. ✪ Try to find an earlier moment in the play where Alfieri speaks about feeling powerless to prevent what is unfolding.

This sense of powerlessness that Alfieri has, his sense that he knows what is about to happen but cannot prevent it, has a dramatic function. In other words, it serves a purpose in terms of the play being a drama that is performed on a stage before an audience. ✪ Can you think what this dramatic purpose might be? An answer would be that it creates dramatic tension in the audience who come to share the lawyer's sense of foreboding, a word that means worried about what is about to happen.

A husband and wife conversation

(From the middle of p. 67 to top of p. 71, where Catherine enters the apartment.)

- ◆ Marco and Rodolpho have moved upstairs to another apartment.
- ◆ Beatrice expresses her unhappiness about all that has happened.
- ◆ Eddie tells Beatrice not to bring up again the fact that they no longer make love.
- ◆ Beatrice tells Eddie that Catherine and Rodolpho are getting married.
- ◆ Beatrice suggests Eddie attends the wedding in order to repair his damaged relationship with Catherine.

Eddie's and Beatrice's marriage is now in a strained state. When Eddie first enters the apartment and asks where everyone is, Beatrice does not answer. Recent events have taken their toll on her feelings and she is emotionally wearied by her husband's irrational behaviour. At first she expresses her feelings openly, '*I don't wanna hear no more about it, you understand? Nothin',*' and her annoyance is evident when she asks, '*What do you want from me? They've moved out; what do you want now?*'

Beatrice's open annoyance at her husband's behaviour is too much for Eddie to take. He sees himself as the man of the house, the person in charge, and he reprimands her: '*I don't like it! The way you talk to me and the way you look at me.*' He expects to get his own way and expects his wife to obey him. Beatrice, however, continues to express her point of view. She does not confront him as aggressively as she did at the beginning of this scene but when he talks about being responsible for his niece she has an uncomfortable question for him. Without referring directly to the fact that he kissed Rodolpho she nevertheless brings up the matter: '*What you done to him in front of her; you know what I'm talking about.*' Beatrice points out that Catherine has been deeply upset by this and quite reasonably asks whether this is really the behaviour of someone who feels responsible for her. Eddie falls back on his excuse that Rodolpho *ain't right*. This time, however, Beatrice draws back from continuing the discussion. ❂ Why do you think Beatrice is reluctant to continue this discussion about Rodolpho's sexuality? Why do you think she says they will carry on as if nothing had happened? Do you think she might be afraid of where this conversation might lead?

It is Eddie who now refers to sex by telling Beatrice there will no further discussion of their love life, or rather the lack of love in their life. This time Beatrice accepts what he says and simply agrees by saying '*Okay.*' When Eddie accuses her of having changed, Beatrice replies '*I'm no different.*' She is clearly hinting that it is Eddie who has changed and the audience has seen enough to know that she is right.

We learn more about the relationship that existed in the past between Eddie and his niece. Beatrice's remark, '*you kept her a baby, you wouldn't let her go out,*' tells us how possessive Eddie has always been about Catherine. Beatrice had tried to get her husband to adopt a more relaxed attitude towards Catherine, '*I told you a hundred times*', but Eddie has always seen himself as the man in charge of his family and he was able to get his way. Now, as his wife points out, it is too late.

Eddie is overcome with emotion as Beatrice tries to convince him that something can still be salvaged from his relationship with Catherine. Tears come to his eyes and Catherine is heard coming down the stairs to their apartment. He may be upset because he knows that his act of betrayal means he can never again be close to Catherine. He must know how his wife's words are unintentionally ironic in the light of the phone call he has just made. She talks of having a party, *'let's start it off happy,'* and how Catherine still loves him. Eddie knows that very soon the immigration authorities will arrive and then his wife's hopeful words will mean nothing. The audience knows this as well and this creates a strong sense of dramatic irony.

Exercises to think about

? Who tells Eddie that he will be despised if he informs on his wife's cousins and what theme does this relate to? (p. 67)

? What reason does Eddie give to Alfieri for provoking Rodolpho into attacking him? (p. 66)

? How do we know that Catherine was very upset by the incident that occurred when Eddie returned home and found Rodolpho and herself in the apartment? (p. 68)

? What was Beatrice referring to when she says to Eddie, *'I told you a hundred times?'* (p. 70)

The following questions refer to the last scene (from the middle of p. 67 to top of p. 71).

? Match the stage instructions below with the correct explanation.
1 [*looking up at him, wearied with it, and concealing a fear of him*]
2 [*He presses his fingers against his eyes.*]
3 [*He gets up, moves about uneasily, restlessly.*]

A Eddie is in a very emotional state when his wife suggests having a wedding party for Catherine and Rodolpho.
B Beatrice does not admit it to her husband but she has become frightened of him because of his irrational behaviour.
C Eddie is very uncomfortable as he listens to his wife talking about the coming wedding because he knows Rodolpho will soon be arrested by the officers of the Immigration Bureau.

?   In this last scene there are moments of dramatic irony because the audience knows, or suspects, what is about to happen and this gives an ironic edge to what a character says. For each of the lines below explain how or why the irony arises. The first one has been done for you as an example.

- LOUIS: Go bowlin', Eddie?
  EDDIE: No, I'm due home.
  LOUIS: Well, take it easy.

Answer: The words of Louis are ironic because Eddie has just telephoned the Immigration Bureau and he is not in a state to *take it easy*. He cannot relax because he knows what that very soon the authorities will arrive at his apartment.

- EDDIE: You used to be different, Beatrice. You has a whole different way.

- EDDIE: Sometimes you talk like I was a crazy man or sump'm.

- BEATRICE: Well, she's been worried about him bein' picked up; this way he could start to be a citizen.

Take a break before the arrest.

The immigrants are arrested

(From top of p. 71 to the bottom of p. 77.)

◆ Eddie tries, unsuccessfully, to get Catherine to change her mind or at least postpone the wedding.

◆ Eddie is alarmed when he discovers that two other immigrants will be arrested alongside his wife's cousins.

◆ When the immigration officers arrive Catherine and Beatrice realize immediately that Eddie is to blame.

◆ Marco, also realizing Eddie is to blame, spits into his face and publicly accuses him of having betrayed them to the authorities.

Beatrice is anxious to try to reconcile Eddie with Catherine but she virtually has to hold Eddie back from

leaving the apartment: [*He starts to go and she holds him.*]
Catherine does invite Eddie to her wedding but her language is
abrupt and impersonal. Her invitation is announced in a way
that suggests she has neither forgotten nor forgiven Eddie for
his earlier behaviour to Rodolpho: '*I'm gonna get married,
Eddie. So if you wanna come, the wedding be on Saturday.*'
When Eddie tries to defend his earlier behaviour by saying he
only wanted the best for her, Catherine replies with one word,
'*Okay,*' and turns to leave the room straight away.

Eddie calls Catherine back in the vain hope that he can
change her mind. He half-apologizes for not having given her
more freedom in the time before the cousins arrived. He tells
her she might meet someone else for, after all, Rodolpho is the
first person she has gone out with. Catherine's replies are short
and decisive. She tells him twice that her mind is made up.
✪ How do you think Catherine is feeling at this moment? Do
you think she is being cruel to Eddie, or kind to him, or both
at the same time?

When the immigration officers knock on the door we are told
that Catherine [*stands a moment staring at him in a realized
horror.*] ✪ Do you think this means Catherine is horrified at the
realization that Rodolpho is going to be arrested or is she
horrified because she has realized Eddie has informed on him?
Could her sense of horror come from both realizations at the
same time?

Notice how Beatrice reacts when the knock comes on
the door. Like her niece, she does not say anything but
the stage instructions inform us what happens on the stage:
[*EDDIE turns, looks at BEATRICE.*] *She sits.* Beatrice understands
immediately that her own husband is responsible for the
arrival of the men from the Immigration Bureau. This is made
even clearer when, as the men walk into the apartment, Eddie
looks at his wife once again and this time the stage instructions
tell us that she [*turns her head away.*]

Eddie reacts to his wife's behaviour by becoming angry with
her and demanding to know what is the matter with her. When
she sees the fear in his face, she too is struck with fear and the
stage instructions make this clear: [*weakened with fear*]: '*Oh,
Jesus, Eddie.*' She covers her face with her hands because, in a

way, she cannot bear to know what her own husband has done. However, she does speak to him – '*My God, what did you do?*' – and the stage instructions accompanying these words are interesting: [– *her final thrust is to turn towards him instead of running from him*]. This suggests that in the crisis that is happening she will not desert her husband. However, this does not take anything away from the shock and horror she is experiencing at the realization of what he has done.

The officers from the Immigration Bureau are instruments of the law and they are immune to the pleas of Catherine and Beatrice for mercy. The fact that they speak in Italian at one stage suggests that they might even be Italian themselves – or are at least used to Italians, but they are not affected by Beatrice's emotional appeal to think about what drove them to leave their own country: '*Who're they hurtin'...They're starving over there.*' Unlike Alfieri, who can acknowledge that some laws are not just, these men do not express an opinion.

Marco's act of spitting in Eddie's face is a powerful dramatic moment. Like many such moments in *A View from the Bridge* it is conveyed by action rather than words. The act of spitting is more than just Marco's expression of contempt for Eddie himself; it is also an act that registers contempt for Eddie's breaking of the social code. By informing to the Immigration Bureau a social taboo has been broken and the act of spitting conveys Marco's identification of Eddie as the culprit.

Eddie reacts to this act by getting extremely annoyed and threatening to kill Marco. In one sense Eddie can be seen to be acting here, pretending to be angry in order to convince people that he is innocent of the accusation. Remember that the end of this scene takes place in the street and members of the local community are watching. ❂ Jog your memory and remind yourself what happened to Vinny Bolzano after he informed on the authorities.

Marco's final words before being led away spell out just how awful will be the consequences of Eddie's act: '*That one! He killed my children! That one stole the food from my children!*' This helps us to appreciate why Vinny's family reacted the way they did. It also helps the audience to realize why Beatrice sat down in silence when she realized what her husband had done. Finally, it helps us to understand the fear that has gripped Eddie in the face of knowing that Marco has publicly identified him as the culprit.

Try to picture Eddie's behaviour on the stage as this scene draws to a close. Lipari and his wife, whose nephew has also been arrested, turn their backs on Eddie and walk away. Eddie follows them up the street proclaiming his innocence. Then he turns to Louis and Mike but they too turn their backs and walk away. Eddie goes after them calling desperately. Talk of death hangs uneasily in the air as Eddie calls out *'I'll kill him! I'll kill him!'* and the stage lights go out.

Marco is released on bail

(Bottom of p. 77 to the top of p. 80, [*The lights dim out*].)

◆ Alfieri waits for Marco's promise that, if released on bail, he will not harm Eddie.

◆ Marco reluctantly gives his promise.

Marco's alarming comment, *'In my country he would be dead now. He would not live this long,'* draws our attention to the strict social code that Marco lives by. According to this code, Eddie has committed a crime which is punishable by death. This also reminds us of the theme of justice and the law that runs through the play. Eddie, by causing Marco to lose his means of providing for his family, is seen to have committed a crime against society. The punishment for this crime will be administered not by the law but by the community. In this way justice will be achieved.

Alfieri is understandably concerned that Marco will take upon himself the task of seeing that justice is obtained. Catherine tries to persuade him that justice will be achieved in a less drastic manner and that killing him is not necessary. *'Nobody is gonna talk to him again if he lives to a hundred.'* There is no reason to think that Catherine is exaggerating when she states this because the audience has already seen how Lipari and others have turned away from him, refusing to speak or acknowledge him.

For Marco, however, simply refusing to speak to someone who has behaved in the way Eddie has is not sufficient punishment: *'Then what is done with such a man?'* Marco asks this question because he cannot believe that the community would settle for such a punishment. Where Marco comes from, justice is swiftly delivered and expected by the community. It is this expectation of seeing justice achieved that makes him say that to promise not to harm Eddie would be *dishonourable*.

The way in which the theme of justice and the law overlaps in this scene with the theme of a social code was first introduced at the beginning of the play.
❂ Which character in the play first introduced both of these themes? The answer to this question is found in words like these spoken by Alfieri at the beginning of the play: *'Oh, there were many here who were justly shot by unjust men. Justice is very important here.'*

The dream that brought Marco to America has now turned into a nightmare. He came to New York in the expectation that employment as a longshoreman would secure a decent living for his family back in Italy. He had planned to work for a couple of years and then return to Italy to be reunited happily with his family. All this has been destroyed and the American Dream has been shattered: *'He degraded my brother. My blood. He robbed my children, he mocks my work. I work to come here, mister!'*

The crisis is approaching

(Top of p. 80 to the middle of p. 81, [*Enter RODOLPHO*].)
◆ Beatrice prepares to leave for Catherine's wedding.
◆ Eddie makes Beatrice choose between staying with him or going to the wedding.
◆ Catherine gets angry and tells Eddie what she now thinks of him.

Eddie forces his wife to choose between staying in the apartment or going to the wedding. It is a choice between her loyalty and love for her husband and her understandable wish to attend the wedding of her orphan niece. Beatrice does not hesitate and she chooses to stay with her husband. It is not a choice she wants to make but when forced to choose she knows what she will do. The relationship between Eddie and Beatrice has survived.

The relationship between Eddie and Catherine, by contrast, has not survived. The last time that the three of them were together was when Beatrice was hoping to persuade Eddie to attend the wedding. Looking back at that scene (p. 71) it is noticeable that Catherine managed to maintain a polite tone of voice when speaking to Eddie, even though it might have been difficult for her. At this stage, however, she can no longer maintain an air of politeness and when she hears Eddie forcing his wife to make a painful choice she finally lets out her feelings. She calls him a *rat*, says that he *belongs in the sewer*, and tearfully expresses how she now sees him: '*He bites people when they sleep! … In the garbage he belongs!*' The warm and loving relationship that Catherine once had for Eddie is gone forever. This is part of the play's tragedy.

When Catherine says that Eddie belongs in the garbage, Beatrice's reply is interesting: '*Then we all belong in the garbage. You and me too.*' She is saying that all three of them bear the responsibility for what has taken place. She does not explain what she means but she is suggesting that Catherine and herself must bear some of the blame because they allowed an unhealthy relationship to develop between Eddie and Catherine. Beatrice saw her husband's possessiveness for Catherine but she never actually did anything to prevent it until it was too late. Look back to the scene in Act 1 (discussed on page 40) where Beatrice told Catherine to stop behaving like a baby. ✪ Do you think it might have turned out differently if Beatrice had given this advice a year or two earlier?

In her anger Catherine spells out the future for Eddie: '*You got no more right to tell nobody nothin'!*' Eddie has been socially branded as someone who broke the rules and the result is that he longer has any rights within the community. When Catherine calls him *Nobody!* she is referring to the price he will have to pay for his behaviour.

He has been rejected by the community and will no longer be recognized as a member of that society. He will become a nobody, a person deprived of a social identity.

Eddie is fully aware of what Catherine is saying and, in one way, she did not need to tell him because he is only too aware of this. Eddie demands that Marco come to the apartment and apologize to him because this would be a way for him to regain his social identity. By apologizing, Marco would be announcing that he made a mistake in identifying Eddie as the person who made the phone call.

I want my name

(Middle of p. 81 to the end of Act 2.)
◆ Rodolpho arrives with the warning that Marco is on his way to the apartment.
◆ Rodolpho apologizes but Eddie is only interested in an apology from Marco.
◆ Eddie and Marco fight and Eddie is killed with the knife he tried to use.
◆ Alfieri mourns the death of Eddie.

Beatrice tries to get her husband to leave with her before Marco arrives but Eddie replies *'Where? Where am I goin'?'* In a sense, Eddie has nowhere to go. He has been disowned by his community for breaking the social code and now Marco is coming to the man's own apartment to seek revenge and justice. Everyone assumes that Marco is right in accusing Eddie but there is no actual evidence for this. ❷ Do you find it believable that everyone would assume Marco is correct? Or do you think it is justified in dramatic terms, in the sense that at this stage in the unfolding drama it is not necessary to account for Marco's reasons for behaving the way he does?

Rodolpho's apology is useless to Eddie because it will not give him back his name. This is the important distinction that Eddie now draws between his wife's two cousins. Referring to Rodolpho, he says *'He didn't take my name.'* Marco, by spitting in his face and publicly accusing him of informing the Immigration Bureau, has robbed Eddie of his social identity.

This is why he now insists that Marco must *give it back to me in front of this neighbourhood*. He goes on to say that whatever Rodolpho might say *don't mean nothin' to nobody!* What counts is the judgement of the community and Rodolpho's opinion will not be decisive in this respect. It was Marco who accused Eddie and it is only Marco who could redeem Eddie's reputation.

 Beatrice confronts her husband with the truth about his feelings for Catherine. She hopes, perhaps, that by spelling out the truth her husband will not persist in his determination to face Marco. *'You want somethin' else, Eddie, and you can never have her!'* This is a highly dramatic moment and both Eddie and Catherine are shocked by her statement.

Beatrice is desperate to save her husband and tells him what the audience has long suspected. Behind Eddie's possessiveness for Catherine lay an unacknowledged sexual attraction. This does not mean, however, that Eddie is not serious about wanting his name back or that he is using it as an excuse to disguise what he really wants. It is part of the play's complexity and its success that the theme of Eddie's relationship with Catherine now overlaps with the theme of a social code.

Eddie's last speech is to members of his own community. He is addressing the society that has rejected him and he insists that Marco has unfairly accused him. We all know that Marco's accusation is a just one but this does not prevent us from being moved by Eddie's plight. He is fighting for his life, not only in the sense that Marco may physically kill him but in the sense that his social identity has been taken away and this is so important to him that he will risk his life to try to regain some respect from the community.

STYLE AND LANGUAGE

The play ends, as it began, with the words of Alfieri. He returns to the idea that *now we settle for half and I like it better* but goes on to speak of Eddie's fate as revealing something that strangely moves him. He says how *'he allowed himself to be wholly known and for that I think I will love him more than all my sensible clients.'* Alfieri is admitting to be moved by someone who did not hide his own nature, even if the feelings that are brought to the surface are uncomfortable ones. Although Alfieri is saying this as a character in the play, the lawyer to whom Eddie came for advice about the law, he is also speaking as someone who stands above the action and is able to comment on it from the outside.

The style of Alfieri's language, when he addresses the audience, has always been different from that of the other characters. The only time that Alfieri speaks like a New Yorker is when he becomes directly involved in the action. Now, however, in the concluding words of the play he speaks as someone who draws conclusions from all that has happened: *'And yet, it is better to settle for half, it must be!'* The audience will agree with him because it would obviously have been better if Eddie could have controlled his feelings. But Alfieri is also moved by the story of someone who could not hide what he really felt and who eventually believed he had no choice but to risk his life in order to try to regain some respect from his society.

The play is over. Do you want your break before or after these exercises?

Boost your learning

? Each of the following lines touches on one of the themes running through the play. Identify the theme and explain briefly how the line relates to the theme.

- BEATRICE: Who're they hurtin', for God's sake, what do you want from them? They're starvin' over there.
- MARCO: That one! I accuse that one!
- EDDIE: He didn't take my name; he's only a punk. Marco's got my name.
- BEATRICE: I'm telling you the truth – tell her good-bye for ever!

? Provide support for the following statements by pinpointing a line or a stage instruction in the play.
- Beatrice is one of the first to realize that Eddie has informed on her cousins, and she is speechless with shock.
- It is spelt out how Eddie's act of betrayal will affect Eddie's family.
- The community turns its back on Eddie.
- Marco cannot understand why the law cannot punish Eddie for what he has done.
- Eddie cannot run away from Marco because he has nowhere to go.

? Register the degree of certainty you attach to your personal response by placing the number somewhere between the two extremes for each of the statements given below. If, for example, you almost agree completely with the first statement then place 1 somewhere towards the left end of the line. If you find it difficult to make up your mind, place the number in the centre of the line.

Agree ————————————————————— Disagree

1 Catherine should not have called Eddie a rat because it hurt his feelings too much.
2 Beatrice should have stood up to Eddie and insisted on going to the wedding.
3 Eddie never admits the truth to himself about how he feels about Catherine.
4 Eddie deserves what he gets because he knew what he was doing.
5 Alfieri is right, there is something *pure* about Eddie Carbone.

? The following list covers nine main episodes in Act 2 but they are not in the correct order. Try to re-order them without looking at the play and then check your answer. Make any necessary corrections so that you end up with a list in the correct order.

- Returning home, Eddie finds Catherine and Rodolpho alone.
- Confrontation for the last time between Marco and Eddie.
- The lawyer Alfieri is visited by Eddie for the second time.
- Arguments between Eddie, Beatrice and Catherine on the day of the wedding.
- Phone call to the Immigration Bureau by Eddie.
- Events are discussed by Eddie and Beatrice but Beatrice doesn't know Eddie has just made the phone call.
- Immigration Bureau officers arrive.
- Beatrice tries to bring Eddie and Catherine together.
- Released on bail, Marco is free to come after Eddie.

A mnemonic that might help:
Red Lines Painted Every Ten Inches Register All Cars

TOPICS FOR DISCUSSION AND BRAINSTORMING

One of the best ways to revise is with one or more friends. Even if you're with someone who hardly knows the text you're studying, you'll find that having to explain things to your friend will help you to organize your own thoughts and memorize key points. If you're with someone who has studied the text, you'll find that the things you can't remember are different from the things your friend can't remember – so you'll help each other.

Discussion will also help you to develop interesting new ideas that perhaps neither of you would have had alone. Use a **brainstorming** approach to tackle any of the topics listed below. Allow yourself to share whatever ideas come into your head – however silly they seem. This will get you thinking creatively.

Whether alone or with a friend, use Mind Mapping (see p. vi) to help you brainstorm and organize your ideas. If with a friend, use a large sheet of paper and thick coloured pens.

TOPICS

Any of the topics below could feature in an exam paper, but even if you think you've found one in your actual exam, be sure to answer the precise question given.

1 Look at the following scenes where Alfieri speaks to the audience about what is to happen. There is the first scene in the play, the scene just before the arrival of the cousins (p. 26), the scene just before Eddie visits Alfieri (p. 45) and the scene just after he has left (p. 50), the scene just before Eddie visits Alfieri for the second time (p. 65), and the final scene after Eddie's death. Find examples of the way Alfieri speaks differently from the other characters. What does he tell us about Eddie? How does he create the feeling that there is something inevitable about what is going to happen?

2 Look at the first scene that brings Eddie, Beatrice and Catherine together (p. 13 to p. 25). Make a list of all the things they say that take on a special meaning in the light of what will happen later. For example, Eddie advises Catherine

(top of p. 15) to remember that she is a young woman now who needs to watch how she behaves. This is what Beatrice will later advise her to do with regard to Eddie himself (p. 44).

3 Look at the scene where Beatrice advises Catherine to modify her behaviour towards Eddie (p. 42 to top of p. 45). Does it help us to understand why Eddie has become too attached to Catherine? What does it tell us about Catherine's feelings at this stage in the play?

4 Compare the first scene where Eddie visits Alfieri for legal advice (p. 45 to p. 49) with the second one (p. 65 to p. 67). What has happened in between these two scenes? What does Alfieri say that is the same and what is new about his advice on the second occasion? How has Eddie changed between the first and second visits?

5 Look at the three dramatic incidents that bring Act 1 to a close: Catherine and Rodolpho dancing, the boxing lesson, and the chair-lifting contest. For each incident, discuss what it tells the audience. In particular, what does each incident tell us that is new?

6 Compare the three scenes where Beatrice and Eddie are alone together. The first short scene is when Catherine is in the kitchen (p. 20), the second is on the street before Catherine returns home late (p. 34 to p. 36) and the third is after the cousins have moved upstairs (p. 68 to p. 70). What does each scene tell us about the relationship between Beatrice and Eddie? How has Eddie changed in the last two scenes?

7 Look again at the conclusion to the play (p. 83 to the end). How do you feel about Eddie as he goes out to meet Marco? Do you find it tragic or does Eddie deserve what happens to him?

8 The play on a postcard. Imagine you are writing to the author, having just read his play. You have exactly 50 words to sum up your impression of the play. Fill in the postcard on page 73.

In all your study, in coursework, and in exams, be aware of the following:

- **Characterization** – the characters and how we know about them (e.g. what they say and do, how they are described), their relationships, and how they develop.
- **Plot and structure** – what happens and how it is organized into different scenes.
- **Setting and atmosphere** – the changing scene and how it reflects the story (e.g. the role of Alfieri in creating a mood for what is about to happen).
- **Style and language** – the author's choice of words and how different characters speak in different ways (e.g. Alfieri, Eddie and Rodolpho have different styles of speaking).
- **Viewpoint** – how the story is told (e.g. through a narrator, through dialogue and action on the stage).
- **Social and historical context** – influences on the author (see 'Background' in this guide).

Develop your ability to:

- Relate **detail** to **broader context, meaning** and **style**.
- Show understanding of the author's **intentions, technique** and **meaning** (brief and appropriate comparisons with other works by the same author will gain marks).
- Give **personal response** and **interpretation**, backed up by **examples** and short **quotations**. (Use short, appropriate quotations as 'evidence' of your understanding of that part of the text – don't just stick large chunks down for the sake of it!)
- **Evaluate** the author's achievement (how far does the author succeed and why?)
- Use literary terms to show your understanding of what the author is trying to achieve with language.

Planning

You will probably have about an hour for one essay. It is worth spending about ten minutes planning it. An excellent way to do this is in the three stages below.

1 **Mind Map** your ideas, without worrying about their order yet.
2 **Order** the relevant ideas (the ones that really relate to the question) by numbering them in the order in which you will write the essay.
3 **Gather** your evidence and short quotes.

You could remember this as the **MOG** technique.

Then write the essay, allowing five minutes at the end for checking relevance, and spelling, grammar and punctuation. **Stick to the question**, and always **back up** your points with evidence in the form of examples and short quotations. Note: you can use '. . .' for unimportant words missed out in a quotation.

Model answer and plan

The next (and final) chapter consists of a model answer to an exam question on *A View from the Bridge*, together with the Mind Map and essay plan used to write it. Don't be put off if you don't think you could write an essay to this standard yet. You'll develop your skills if you work at them. Even if you're reading this the night before the exam, you can easily memorize the MOG technique in order to do your personal best.

The model answer and essay plan are good examples to follow, but don't try learn them off by heart. It's better to pay close attention to the wording of the question you choose to answer in the exam, and allow Mind Mapping to help you to think creatively.

Before reading the answer, you might like to do a plan of your own, then compare it with the example. The numbered points, with comments at the end, show why it's a good answer.

QUESTION

How does Eddie behave as a husband and what is his attitude to Catherine?

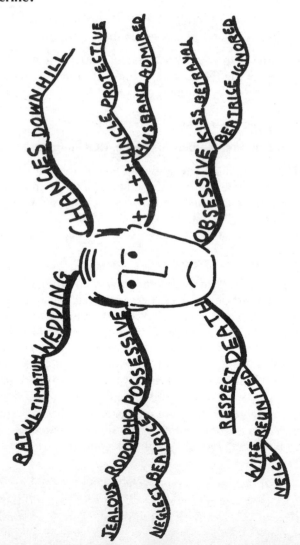

CHANGES DOWNHILL

++ UNCLE PROTECTIVE

++ HUSBAND ADMIRER

OBSESSIVE KISS BETRAYAL

BEATRICE IGNORED

RAT ULTIMATUM WEDDING

JEALOUS RODOLPHO POSSESSIVE

NEGLECTS BEATRICE

RESPECT DEATH

WIFE REUNITED

NEICE

PLAN

1 Changes in behaviour in course of the play – closely linked with his attitude to Catherine.
2 Good husband and caring uncle – at beginning of the play.
3 Possessive attitude to Catherine – reaction to Rodolpho.
4 Changing behaviour as husband – Beatrice's concern.
5 Obsessive attitude to Catherine – becomes irrational.
6 Final scenes – attitude to wife and Catherine.
7 Conclusion – tragedy of a good husband destroyed by his feelings for Catherine.

ESSAY

In the course of the play Eddie's behaviour as a husband changes and develops, and the changes are closely linked with his attitude to Catherine. At the beginning of the play we see a good husband and a protective and caring uncle. However, Catherine is becoming a young woman and the arrival of Rodolpho brings to the surface the unpleasant aspect of Eddie's attitude to his niece. This, in turn, affects his relationship with his wife and eventually Eddie's positive role as a husband and uncle is destroyed in a downhill progression.[1]

In the scene at the beginning of the play, before the cousins arrive, we get a sense of a reasonably happy family life. Eddie sees himself in the traditional role as the head of an Italian-American family. He likes to be in charge but he does not seem cruel or selfish. He considers it an honour to help his wife's cousins and Beatrice is tearfully proud of her husband's behaviour. She takes his face in her hands and says to Catherine, 'You see what he is? Mmm! You're an angel!'[2] Eddie's attitude towards Catherine is a very protective one and he is dismayed at the thought of her leaving school and joining the adult world. We sense that he is over-protective but after a conversation with Beatrice he agrees to Catherine going out to work. We sense some apprehension on the part of Beatrice but they seem able to deal with one another in an amicable way.[3]

Rodolpho's arrival brings out Eddie's possessive attitude towards his niece. He takes an immediate, jealous dislike to Rodolpho when he sees him winning Catherine's affections. He convinces himself that the young man is effeminate and homosexual and he tries to convince Beatrice likewise.

Beatrice's response, 'you crazy or sump'm', will turn out to be closer to the truth that she would like because Eddie does become increasingly irrational in his behaviour. Even at this stage we suspect that Edide's attitude towards Catherine is affecting his relationship with his wife: 'When am I gonna be a wife again, Eddie?' Beatrice's question, and her husband's refusal to discuss his neglect of their love life, tells us that all is not well between them. Eddie is more concerned about Catherine being out late with Rodolpho, and his emotional attitude towards Catherine places a great stress on his relationship with Beatrice.[4]

After the confrontation between Eddie and Rodolpho, at the beginning of Act 2, the changes in Eddie as a husband and as an uncle to Catherine are very apparent. When Catherine is kissed by Eddie it comes as a shock to her to realize that he feels about her in this way. At the end of this scene, when she tells him she is leaving with Rodolpho, Eddie threatens both of them, 'Don't make me do nuttin', Catherine.' She has not seen this irrational hostility in him before, and their relationship is never the same again. The changes in Eddie's behaviour as a husband is shown in the scene that leads up to the arrival of the immigration officers. Beatrice has moved her cousins upstairs in an attempt to reduce the tensions that have been created but this does not satisfy Eddie. He is angry with his wife because she doesn't share his obsessive view of what has taken place. 'I want my respect,' he demands, and he orders her not to bring up the subject of the lack of sex in their relationship. At the beginning of the play Eddie and Beatrice were able to communicate with one another but he cannot see how he has changed. Ironically, he accuses his wife of behaving differently but she truthfully replies, 'I'm no different'. The scene where Beatrice tries to bring Catherine and Eddie together over Catherine's coming wedding shows how uncomfortable Catherine now is in his company. Eddie has not listened to his wife's attempts to make them friends again and he persists in trying to get Catherine to change her mind.[5]

Eddie's behaviour as a husband is especially unpleasant when he refuses to let his wife attend the wedding.[6] His ultimatum forces her to choose between their marriage and her wish to be with Catherine on her wedding day. Behind this show of male authority lies a breakdown in their marriage, even though

Beatrice loyally stands by him. When Catherine hurls abuse at Eddie and calls him a 'rat' the stage instructions tell us that he looks as if he would throw the table at Catherine in his rage. Eddie has bullied his wife into submission and made his niece hate him with real intensity. Their feelings for each other make a very sad comparison with the scene at the beginning when they laughed and joked about spiders.[7]

After Rodolpho warns them about Marco, Eddie is implored by Beatrice to think about what he is doing. She tells him twice that she loves him but he dismisses her and she is forced into being blunt: 'You want somethin' else, Eddie, and you can never have her!' Beatrice knows that it is his attitude to Catherine that has caused the change in his behaviour but her effort to make him see sense is a failure.[8]

Eddie's desire to keep Catherine drives him to an act of betrayal that is seen as a crime by his society. By meeting Marco he hopes to reclaim his identity and regain the respect of his community. This becomes the most important thing in his life and he ignores the desperate pleading of both Beatrice and Catherine.[9] At the moment of death Eddie's thoughts return to his wife and he dies in her arms. There is a reconciliation of sorts between the three of them but the audience is struck by the tragedy of a man who destroyed his relationship with his wife because of his excessive emotional attachment to his niece.[10]

WHAT'S SO GOOD ABOUT IT?

1 Concise introduction, focusing on the question and showing awareness of character development in the play.
2 Awareness of character relationships, backed up by example and quotation.
3 Understanding of plot.
4 Understanding of the link between Eddie as husband and his attitude to Catherine.
5 Relating plot development to the question.
6 Personal response, related to the question.
7 Evaluating the changes in Eddie as a husband and uncle.
8 Understanding of the scene and relating it to the question.
9 Relating to an important theme in the play.
10 Good conclusion that relates events to the essay question.

GLOSSARY OF LITERARY TERMS

alliteration   repetition of a sound at the beginnings of words, e.g. *low over the land.*

chorus   a group of characters who comment on and express feelings about what is happening in the play.

context   the social and historical influences on the author.

dramatic irony   where the audience knows something not known by one or more characters.

foreshadowing   an indirect warning of things to come, often through imagery.

image   a word picture used to make an idea come alive; e.g. a **metaphor**, **simile**, or **personification** (see separate entries).

imagery   the kind of word picture used to make an idea come alive.

irony   (1) where the author or a character says the opposite of what they really think, or pretends ignorance of the true facts, usually for the sake of humour or ridicule; (2) where events turn out in what seems a particularly inappropriate way, as if mocking human effort. (See also **dramatic irony**.)

metaphor   a description of a thing as if it were something essentially different but also in some way similar; e.g. *the gullet of New York swallowing the tonnage of the world.*

personification   a description of a thing as if it were a person; e.g. *the sun was hiding.*

prose   language in which, unlike verse, there is no set number of syllables to a line, and no rhyming.

setting   the place in which the action occurs, usually affecting the atmosphere; e.g. the apartment.

simile a comparison of two things different in most ways but somehow similar; e.g. Alfieri says of Eddie, *His eyes were like tunnels.*

structure the overall pattern of the plot.

theme an idea explored by an author; e.g. marriage.

viewpoint how the story is told; e.g. through action, or in discussion between characters.

INDEX

Act 1
  revision 47–9
  summary 3–6
Act 2
  revision 68–70
  summary 7–8
Alfieri
  character 43, 67–8
  role 14–5, 43, 67–8
  style and language 28–9, 35, 36, 43
  and Eddie 42, 55, 56–7
  and justice and law 27, 42, 55
American Dream 21–2, 30, 31, 35, 50, 64

Beatrice
  character 12, 39
  and Catherine 41, 41–2
  and Eddie 12, 21, 30, 36, 37, 41, 45, 46, 57–8, 61–2, 65, 67, 76–9

Catherine
  character 11
  and Beatrice 41, 41–2
  and Eddie 28, 30, 31, 36, 39, 46, 50, 51–2, 56, 57–8, 61, 64–5
  and Rodolpho 12, 35, 46, 50
chorus 15, 80

dramatic irony 38, 60, 80
dramatic tension 43

Eddie
  character 9–10, 38
  and Beatrice 33, 36, 37, 41, 57–8, 61–2, 67, 76–9
  and Catherine 28, 30, 31, 36, 39, 46, 51–2, 54, 56, 57–8, 61, 64–5, 65, 67, 76–9
  and justice and law 14, 18–9, 27, 32, 42, 55, 62, 63–4
  and Marco 46, 62–3

  and Rodolpho 36, 37, 43, 46, 52, 54, 66
  and social codes 55–6, 62, 65–6, 66, 67
  and Vinny Bolzano 10

Greek tragedy 15

Louis and Mike 38

Marco
  character 14
  chair-lifting 46–7
  and American Dream 35, 64
  and Eddie 46, 62–3
  and justice and law 64
  and social codes 45, 63
marriage 20–1, 30, 33, 37, 41, 45, 46, 50, 56, 57, 61, 64, 65
Mind Maps
  model answers and essay plan 76
  themes 18, 25
  who's who 17

parental role 19–20, 30, 31, 32, 36, 37, 39, 41, 43, 45, 46, 51, 54, 58, 60–1, 65

Rodolpho
  character 13, 40
  language 51
  and American Dream 35, 50
  and Catherine 12, 35, 45, 46
  and Eddie 36, 37, 43, 46, 50, 52, 66
  and social codes 35

social codes 10, 14, 22–4, 27, 32, 35, 38, 45, 55, 62, 63, 64, 65, 66
style and language 28, 33, 35, 36, 38, 41–2, 43, 46, 51, 52, 56, 67–8

Vinny Bolzano 10, 23, 32

BUZAN TRAINING COURSES

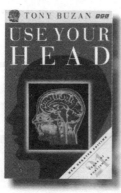